DIM SUM STORIES FROM THE HEART

MY CRAZY ADVENTURES FROM HONG KONG TO AUSTRALIA AND EVERYWHERE IN BETWEEN

CHUPING YU

TESTIMONIALS

Yum char dim sum is one of the best culinary cultural imports from China. For New Zealand and Australia, Chu Ping Yu is another valuable cultural and colourful addition. Digest these delicious vignettes, laugh, learn, and think about the extraordinary exploits of this mature Chiwi (a Chinese kiwi). ChuPing did hippie counterculture at its very beginnings.

She did fusion cooking before it was a thing, and she has amalgamated her physical and soul healing into her own philosophy of life. In these pages read some of the most insightful and funny travel stories I've ever come across. Follow ChuPing on her journey through home, mothering, marriage, and liberation.

There is something here for everybody. As she says, dim sum is to be shared and enjoyed with good conversations. I hope these stories converse with your heart and give you plenty to ruminate throughout your day. Congratulations ChuPing for sharing your life with us.

Sue Lytollis (Raukawa, Tainui) is known as the modern founder of women's self-defence in Aotearoa for which she received QSM in 1995. She has known ChuPing since the 90s.

ChuPing joined the Choir of Hard Knocks in 2008 (six months after it started) and has been the most wonderful member of our 'choir family' ever since. Always radiating positivity and a beautiful smile, I know how much the choir and our music-making have meant to her personal journey for the past 15 years.

I've also been blessed to be the recipient of some of ChuPing's amazing cooking skills, and her combination of singing and food has been such a gift to us, as well as part of her own personal healing.

**Jonathan Welch,
AM Founding Artistic Director
Choir of Hard Knocks**

Firstly, I would like to congratulate ChuPing on writing her first book. It is a big task but ChuPing has done extremely well and should be very proud of herself.

I found ChuPing's book very interesting and have thoroughly enjoyed all the wonderful stories she shares from her life and travels. The interesting changes in her life had me captivated from the very beginning of the book.

I especially enjoyed reading about her experiences living off the land in New Zealand and found myself there with her in my mind. It seemed like a very interesting time for her.

Congratulations ChuPing on a wonderful book that so many will enjoy and learn about things we may not ever have a chance to learn about ourselves.

Julie Fisher – Author

ChuPing Yu has been a trusted associate for almost two decades. Her extraordinary talents have been seen and appreciated by many and these have included delectable cooking feats, intuitive thinking and advice, special artwork and now her love of storytelling. ChuPing is a modest lovable person, always appearing cheerful with a warm smile, eager to be there and help anybody at any time. I am proud to call her my friend.

Suzy Rideout – Spiritual Mentor

First published by Ultimate World Publishing 2023
Copyright © 2023 ChuPing Yu

ISBN

Paperback: 978-1-922828-83-5
Ebook: 978-1-922828-84-2

ChuPing Yu has asserted her rights under the Copyright, Designs and Patents Act 1988 to be identified as the author of this work. The information in this book is based on the author's experiences and opinions. The publisher specifically disclaims responsibility for any adverse consequences which may result from use of the information contained herein. Permission to use information has been sought by the author. Any breaches will be rectified in further editions of the book.

All rights reserved. No part of this publication may be reproduced, stored in or introduced into a retrieval system, or transmitted in any form, or by any means (electronic, mechanical, photocopying, recording or otherwise) without the prior written permission of the author. Any person who does any unauthorised act in relation to this publication may be liable to criminal prosecution and civil claims for damages. Enquiries should be made through the publisher.

Cover design: Ultimate World Publishing
Layout and typesetting: Ultimate World Publishing
Editor: Rebecca Low

Ultimate World Publishing
Diamond Creek,
Victoria Australia 3089
www.writeabook.com.au

DEDICATION AND DEVOTION

Dedication and Devotion, to me, this combination is where I base my spiritual exploration of SELF. This is where my strong feelings of LOVE, loyalty, and the willingness to give a lot of time and energy to what I feel passionate about. My fascination is to explore my inner and outer world at soul level.

Often, devotion is associated with some form of religion, not as religious worship. I follow a devotion of Buddhist teachings and from a young age, had an inquisitive nature to seek and experience life with people who seem happy. I went to investigate a church that a friend from high school invited me to, where I saw people speaking in tongues. It didn't resonate. On my return to the city after my time as a devotee to a guru, I attended a spiritual church, that focused more on spiritualism than religion. Channelling and psychic mediumship are practiced. There, I met my Māori spiritual teachers.

As a Chinese Kiwi, I was accepted and embraced by the Māori culture and adopted into tribal traditions when welcomed onto a Marae—a traditional meeting house. It was a new world to me.

From a young age, I started to immerse myself in the Māori culture. In primary school, I felt bold and was always put in the front with the singing for the gala days. I had my chin painted with the traditional tattoo, much like the Indian henna that gets painted on hands for special celebrations.

The traditional welcome is sung like a song, like a blessing or invitation, in a way. The first time I heard the Powhiri (prayer) Waiata and the Kapa Haka, the sounds embraced and connected with my soul, birthing a new sense of spirituality, which I adopted.

So, when I moved to Australia and witnessed my first Welcome to Country ceremony, my heart was opened, in a sense. I felt a strong sense of fitting in, like I made the right choice. It was very affirming.

Therefore, I would like to show my respect and acknowledgement of the Aboriginal people of Australia, a place that has been my home since 2008.

I would like to acknowledge the Wurundjeri people who are the traditional custodians of this land. I would like to pay respect to the elders, both past and present, of the Kulin Nation and extend respect to other Indigenous Australians present.

CONTENTS

TESTIMONIALS	III
DEDICATION AND DEVOTION	VII
INTRODUCTION	1
EARLY BEGINNINGS	5
MUSIC NIGHT	15
BETWEEN TWO WORLDS	25
FROM NO JOB TO TWO JOBS	43
HAPPY BIRTHDAY	47
IN THE BEGINNING	53
MY PAWPAW	59
NEW COMPUTER: MY NEW LIFE TO BECOME A WRITER	63
RECONNECTING WITH A LONG, FORGOTTEN FRIEND	67
COMING HOME AND THE CHANGE OF LIFE	71
ANOTHER TRIP	77
FEELING THE FEAR	81
MY TRIP TO WEST FOOTSCRAY LIBRARY	85

HEART FELT LIKE A MAORI	87
WOMAN WARRIOR	93
EATING MY WAY AROUND THE WORLD IN ONE DAY	99
THE VIRTUAL WORLD	101
FUK LUK SAU	103
ODE TO LOVE	117
WALKING ON BROKEN GLASS	123
BOURKE STREET MALL DISASTER AVOIDED	127
LIBRARY LOVERS' DAY	131
LIGHTING OF CANDLES	133
LIVING OFF THE SMELL OF AN OILY RAG	139
LOVE AND NEW UNDERSTANDINGS	143
COOKING IN GREECE	149
SANCTUARY	153
THE PERFECT GIFT	159
COVID BIRTHDAY BLUES	163
SELF-ABSORPTION TO SELF AWARENESS	169
HUNTING AND GATHERING	171
TIME FOR A RECIPE	175
TIPS AND TRICKS	177
CHINESE DUMPLINGS	183
CRAVINGS	187
BEST COFFEE EVER	191
MORE THAN ONE MOTHER	195
AFTERWORD	199
ABOUT THE AUTHOR	201
ACKNOWLEDGEMENTS	203

INTRODUCTION

The translation of 'dim sum' in English is 'point to the heart'. Dim sum dishes are small little bites, which are the ultimate comfort food in many other cultures, but they have a Cantonese origin. This inspired the name of my book, *Dim Sum Stories*, as it's a collection of short stories from my heart.

Another important term to note is 'yum-char', which translates to 'drink tea'. It is a traditional brunch that consists of tea and dim sum enjoyed by many people of many cultures around the world. It was started in traditional tea houses and restaurants, enjoyed either as brunch or lunch.

My first cooking experience as a teacher was a weekend, introducing yum char with different dim sum, Chinese dumplings, and steamed buns. This two-day class was the foundation of my cooking career in the early 1990s.

It was in a small country town called Karamea in New Zealand, around two and a half hours drive from where I lived at the time.

For me and many, dim sum is the ultimate comfort food. In those days, it was only offered in the big main cities, certainly unknown in a small country town like Karamea, which barely consisted of 300 people, since it was a farming community.

HOW IT ALL STARTED or ABOUT THE CULTURE

The dim sum culture is a tradition that has set roots in China and has spread worldwide. I was surprised and amazed to come across a Chinese tea house offering yum char in Cancun, Mexico while holidaying there a few years ago.

Each dish at yum char is a small serving of tasty treats, which is why I chose this title for my first book. Each story is a small share that comes from my heart, and as each serving is small, you can have many. I believe sushi trains were an idea that could have stemmed from yum char.

A few proper dining etiquettes for a yum-char.

1. Serve everyone else before yourself.

2. Never hog and lay claim to one dish, share.

Introduction

3. Use a serving spoon or an extra pair of chopsticks, for serving. Never use your own that's touched your mouth.

4. Never take the last bite of a dish until others have declined it.

5. Take your time, never rush.

6. Make conversation.

7. Connect with the people you are dining with.

Food tastes much better when you eat with others rather than alone. It's a social event as with more people, there will be a bigger variety of food. I probably have had thousands of yum-chars in my life but have only been to two or three on my own. Eating and sharing food with others is something I have always enjoyed. I've found that there's more to taste in sharing snippets of various dishes. This is something I compared to my life, as seen through my eyes and experiences. I would like to say this book has been 20 years coming as I have always dreamt of writing a book—a cookbook—while I was travelling around the world.

Although this isn't a cookbook, I do share my passion for eating and cooking in my stories. When I first started telling people I was writing this book, they all seemed to jump to the conclusion that it was a cookbook.

A cookbook may still be on the cards in the future, but until then, I've included a few recipes and tips as a tease, and there's another book to follow.

EARLY BEGINNINGS

This story is about my experience, which comes from my perception. I am very personal, and I opened my heart to share my experiences. This story may not resonate with every reader, but my experience will reach open-minded hearts on a deep soul level.

How often do we think and believe we love ourselves, when deep inside, we have so much self-doubt? Can you look at your reflection In the mirror for five minutes? Look into your own eyes, try to stay still and not get distracted with thoughts flashing. Focus and stare into your eyes and think positively. Compliment yourself. Recall nice, lovely things others have said and embrace the vibrations of these words. It's not easy in the beginning. I am sure it will become easier with practice, as I found through my experiences.

I had trouble when I first tried this; sometimes I would get tearful. Crying is very cleansing, and often you will feel much better after a good cry. And, as with doing anything repeatedly, what once was hard gradually becomes easier. You gain confidence.

Nowadays, we look for tools and techniques with meditation to take our minds off billions of thoughts. It is not the formality of making our mind blank, it's about training it to centre on our own inner vibrations, stopping the chitter-chatter of outer influences. We would be lying to ourselves if we said we did not get stressed. It can be subconscious awareness or nonawareness, and we can store stressful emotions without even being aware.

When we make a conclusion about awareness, there are many forms of meditation and tools that suit different souls. It's made easier for some by using a mantra. A mantra is a word or sound made to combat mental cloudiness and change the body's vibrations, also known as a chant or a prayer. For me, it's not always one thing or one way, it's a combination and mix of actions to alter my mind and change my state.

I will share the very first mantra that was given to me. It's a silent chant of "soo-hum". Breathing in for the "soo" and then out for the "hum". Keep repeating this, the vibrations of these sounds transform the mind to a slower calmness and peaceful state. I have found it to be extremely useful in stressful situations and often a great natural pickup remedy. I believe that if we meditate, we become better versions of ourselves.

It has been said that many roads can lead to Rome. It's a phrase meaning there are many paths we can follow to take us to where we want to go, so it's a matter of choices and being open to new opportunities.

I have travelled the world, and there were times when I felt a little lost in direction, but I still ended up on a fascinating journey. I met amazing new people, making unexpected friends. I explored many other ways of living, approaching it from another angle. This was much like my life when I was younger, and that sense of freedom of living life in the moment. I was rebellious and did not want to be the good, little Chinese girl my family wanted and expected me to be.

For me, it's about the road less travelled, especially now. As I get older, I've become more open to accepting non-traditional things and adjusting to what feels right and what doesn't feel right. Then on another level, drawing on old traditions and seeing things from a different angle, I start to see them in a new and different light. For me, not believing in marriage and often seeing it as just a piece of paper, a fleeting emotion disguised as love before the separation. Then doing it again just to end up hating them, the person they claimed to love, seemed so pointless.

I came from a first-generation Chinese family who immigrated to New Zealand when I was around seven years old in 1960. It's not just about the traditions we inherited from our forefathers combined with our current personal values. In being naïve and open-minded, I was constantly open to change. I wouldn't follow the traditions of my hardworking (overworked) parents who were never home. Their thoughts were to give me a home and food on the table; to them, that was all that was required or all they thought was necessary. Times are different now, as the bare necessities are not enough. That's often why there are problems due to a lack of communication, but in most cases, parents and children find it challenging to be open with each other. It's sad, indeed, when parents and children stop communicating with each other, holding onto their old, outdated ideas, instead of meeting somewhere in between to find a happy medium.

The first and only words of English I knew when I arrived in New Zealand were, "Sorry monkey." I do not remember how, as a child, I even knew these two words when we never had TV, and I remember playing with other children, but they didn't speak English. As my family never had any form of introduction to prepare us for entering an English-speaking country, we were thrown into the situation, learning as we went along. This is the reason why I like to wing things rather than make long-term plans that don't come naturally or easily, especially as I get older.

Now, in reverse, English is my chosen first language. I must think in English to speak Cantonese, as my vocabulary is limited to that of a child. In general, Chinese people don't express emotions. I believe my need to communicate regularly is not a so-called normal Chinese way to be.

Some years ago, after I first moved to Melbourne, I was in Hamer Hall where I heard my old Guru speak for the first time since the 1970s. Back then, in 1974, I was 20 years old, and he was 16, and now I was older and he was a man in his 50s. I had to use Google Translate to understand what was being said, and none of what he spoke at Hammer Hall clicked and resonated with me like it did when I was younger. It had been a long time since I'd heard or seen him, and I realised how much I had changed, and he was no longer the young boy he was when I first became his devotee.

I was only 19 when I stumbled across *Divine Light Mission* and Guru Maharaj Ji. His current name is Prem Pal Singh Rawat, and he's an international speaker. He was three or four years younger than me, and the youngest of three sons and successor as the Sat Guru. His father was Maharaja Ji, which means Indian Priest.

My parents thought I was crazy to walk away from my Christian upbringing and become one of the Guru's devotees. My brother jokingly re-named it 'The Fat Boy Club', which was his term of insult at the time. Maharaji

Ji was a chubby teenager of 16 when I joined. When he was 17, he met a slightly older American airline hostess and they fell in love before his devotees gave him his own private plane so he could travel the world and share his teachings. The rumour was that his mother tried to denounce him to give the leadership to his older brother. What a traditional reaction for any parent of any culture. His mother even disowned him for marrying an older 'white' woman.

This was very challenging for my parents, who raised me as an Anglican. During this period of my life, I needed a spiritual mentor. He turned up in the nick of time as all my peers were dabbling in substances that altered mind states. It saved me from forming an addiction to drugs, and it was then that I met the love of my life and blindly followed his path of living as a hippie rather than the path I was on. His name was Roger, and he was born in England and migrated to New Zealand 10 years before me.

When I met Roger, he was a roadie for the then well-known band called *The Pelicans*. There were four band members plus their groupies. All the men had long hair and beards, and it took me some time to tell each guy apart. At such a young age, I was possibly too open. I loved to try new things at the drop of a hat. In hindsight, this became a pattern I repeated and recognised in my later years. I quote a song, "Wise men say, only fools rush in," by Elvis.

Early Beginnings

I followed my heart and gave Satsang to Roger, the love of my life and his friends. Satsang is speaking and sharing the truth. And as I write this, I think I'm giving a form of Satsang in my writing by calling it *Dim Sum Stories* as these are stories from my heart.

To be initiated as a devotee, one had to ask for knowledge. Roger was too intellectual, according to the spiritual teacher who said "no", as he was asking from his head, not his heart. I knew by staying with Roger he would either help me build my devotion and practice to becoming a devotee himself, like me or lead me and take my focus away. It was the latter, I lost focus. The most positive and joyful outcome was bringing two unique and beautiful girls into the world. Becoming a mother at 21 was most challenging as I thought about the responsibilities of being a mother at such a young age alongside not having electricity to bring up two young kids, all by the time I was 23 years old. This made me grow up fast. The daily challenges I braved each day were tough. I taught myself to cook and keep house, something I wasn't shown how to do as my parents were never around—they were workaholics. So, I made it a big point to be there daily for my children, especially after school when they were older.

I was a latch-key kid, which meant having a key to leave for school and return home, caring for my younger sister while being shadowed by my older brother. I focused on doing the best I could at the time, just as my parents did the best they could.

Throughout my life, I felt I may have had despair and depression. I've found this to be because I was torn between two cultures. I learnt that my brutal battles became my most joyful moments. Being a child myself, a young mother, and somewhat naïve, this was incredibly challenging, as we had no electricity for the first 14 years. I was also a vegetarian when I arrived but learnt how to kill meat for Roger. He didn't cook and wanted meat as he was doing heavy manual work at the time.

One day, we were given a box of live little chicks. They were noisy and we had to keep them close to the coal range to keep them warm. They turned out to be all boys, those that understand rearing chickens knows only one rooster can ever rule the flock. Then it became my responsibility to utilize them to feed my family.

I didn't really know how to be a mother as I wasn't really mothered myself. I often regard my daughters as my sisters and as my friends, and in writing this in my 60s as a grandmother, my hashtag is #funkygranny. My hard-learnt lesson is always to keep up communication and ask questions, even if they might sound silly. As the saying goes, "Better to be a fool for one minute than a lifetime of the silence of not knowing," a motto I have adopted. As change is inevitable, we should all constantly remember to be self-loving. I still have lapse moments if I'm not doing my meditation practice daily.

In the past, I have used many forms of oracles, from tarot cards to animal medicine cards. My favourite was the Viking runes well over three decades ago. A quote from these runes is, "First, draw from the well to satisfy our own thirst before we can indeed be able to keep giving to others." So often, as women, we give so much that we can often end up neglecting ourselves until we reach a burnout point.

Pace yourself, often. Living life can be compared to running a marathon. Loving yourself takes training, even if it's only five minutes a day. In doing it consistently, we learn to understand ourselves on a deeper level, like becoming our own best friend.

I take mental health days where I don't pressure myself to do things. On these days, I will spend the day just being, not doing. No schedules, listening to what my body feels like doing. I always feel better after this and realise that when I become stressed, it's time for self-care. It's time to take time for my well-being.

We must also maintain our body by treating it as a temple; our bodies are the vehicles we travel with through life. Sometimes, people treat their cars so much better than their bodies, then wonder why they are in so much pain both inwardly and outwardly. The greatest gift is self-love. Keep moving rather than be stuck in your bodies and minds. Know the joy of becoming your own best friend and learn to maintain your own well-being rather than going to others. Hear your inner voice as it will always guide you to make the right choices.

In one of my favourite books, *The Alchemist*, the main character Santiago travelled the world looking for treasure, looking outwardly, and only found it when he returned home. He finally found what he was in search of for such a long time without realising the treasure he already had. The travelling opened his whole being into another dimension of self-awareness. When he returned home, somehow, the journey changed his perception, awareness and understanding of himself. Travelling can open the mind, the soul, and the heart.

MUSIC NIGHT

The West Coast of NZ for the wild bush and rainy weather. Often stuck indoors with terrible weather and driven by my passion for eating, I started experimenting and adapting ingredients I could source locally. This, in turn, expanded my love for food, eating, and sharing, using my family and neighbours as my guinea pigs. There were no complaints with them often asking when I was cooking again so they could be around to taste my trial runs of new recipes.

Daily cooking on a wood/coal range and using ash and embers in a camp oven were the roots and foundation that harnessed my passion for cooking. My back to basic living wasn't a planned choice—I had a chosen career in fashion design that I abandoned for my love of a man. I knew little about what my new life would be like and had to learn how to cook for him and my first child without any modern conventional tools and methods.

My brain never imagined just how difficult it would be. However, I did it while feeding my passion for food and eating, and found by accident my passion, which turned into a career. I will add that the hard work became more familiar by the time my second child was born.

Failing in love moved me to follow my heart, which was new and exciting, embracing a destiny and future of unknown outcomes. To give up my life as I knew it for this new experience, I honestly would not have pursued it if I know how difficult it would be. But it has been said that we are always wiser after the fact. To live a new lifestyle, I didn't even know existed. Living on the land had—and still is—sometimes romanticised in movies and television shows. I had never even come across the word 'hippie' and fell into an unplanned future of daily challenges in a way of life that was not an easy task.

Daily challenges were…challenging, in many ways. It started when I got up in the darkness of early morning—getting out of bed was the hardest in winter. There was no instant touch to turn on the light switch. It took up to 14 years for a national grid to be installed in the area, and it happened because of a new enterprise. The re-opening of an old, abandoned coal mine on the property next door made it more feasible to install the cable such a long way. Most of the coast had already installed electricity lines but we were some 35 miles away, which is a very long distance for the installation of so many poles. The power lines no longer have to carry a 44 gallon fuel drum to town to bring back for the generator: hallelujah! This business didn't last, though, as the investment turned sour. It was great, electricity was finally installed, though, I wondered If those entrepreneurs hadn't re-open the old coal mine on the neighbouring lot of land if we would have ever had the national electricity at all.

Preparing lamps to light before the sun went down was a difficult task. Not having to light candles and fill kerosene lamps. All the fuel we used had to be transported from town. Sometimes, some was spilled and it's rather a strong scent, like petroleum gasoline. Although, I have not visited Sovereign Hill, from looking at the promotional videos, I think our way of life was very similar to that of the turn of the century early pioneers living on the land in rural areas. Like that of the American colonists of the wild, wild west. Those that watch the TV dramatization, *The Little House on the Prairie* was, 'the days of our lives'. Until national grid electricity came. My hard lifestyle became so much easier. The coal range had a switch installed to the cylinder to have hot water in summer, meaning the coal range didn't need to be going 24/7 anymore.

Every day I had to milk our cows (up to five of them), each giving roughly a gallon of milk. We let the cream settle and skimmed it off the top of the milk to make our own butter. It took around five gallons milked from five cows to make a block of cheese that weighed a little over a kilogram in today's measurement. It was a real labour of love, as the daily chores were very repetitive. Like making the curds in a large pot on The old coal range, then draining off the whey, wrapping the solids in muslin cloth. Using something like a small cake tin with nail holes punched through the bottom and sides to press the solids into a shape, and let the whey drain out. With the whey, I kept making fluffy delicious scones, some with cheese, which was my preference, while Roger preferred sweet ones or plain ones so he could have them with cream and jams I made from cheap seasonal fruit. The larder (pantry) was a pretty and delightful sight, with rows of glass preserving jars displaying my efforts and labours of love.

I have written stories about the daily life and the activities involved. How once we butchered a whole cow, and processed a massive amount of meat, as one cow can weigh up to 1000 pounds. Processing all the meat by corning beef or making salamis tied with twine that hung from the ceiling in the kitchen to dry was all part of the curing process. We took some of the meat to a local butcher in town to make them into sausages. Nowadays, I rarely ever enjoy sausages, as they are so heavily processed, with so many additives. We purchased a freezer and placed it in a friend's garage before the national electricity was installed. This meant we could freeze our own home-grown meat with next to no preservatives. Picking up a pack or two on route home from town.

There was also the hard work of using an old copper, set in a large concrete base with a fire underneath to do the washing and daily boiling of the cotton nappies. This was long before disposable nappies and even when they were available, they were very expensive when my children were young. Being out for the day carrying used and soiled nappies home to clean was just something we had to get used to. Thankfully, the smell didn't seem to be a problem. Maybe it was mainly our homegrown organic diet or the fact it was 40-some years ago.

I lived as an early-year pioneer by learning new experiences from daily chores that took most of the day. I was making it easier to get more innovative by stomping on the cotton nappies in the bath—a classic old claw foot bathtub—an idea I got from old fashion traditional winemaking after reading about grape-stomping. I also made my bread by grinding (by hand) the whole wheat into flour, preparing the correct amount of yeast to raise the bread, kneading, and then baking the bread in the coal range oven.

Life was a mixture of adventure and struggle, under the umbrella of love and being young—a simple life of hardship and happiness. It was often just repetitive and other times filled with joy and festivities.

On the farm, I was living a simple life. At times it felt like just continuously ongoing hard work and at other times, pure happiness, like a balancing act on a seesaw. The highs and the lows seemed like an emotional rollercoaster, and often just repetitive with endless chores and other times of festivity celebrations, always walking on a thin line of highs and lows. I unfolded a passion and skill in my love of cooking. My parents were never around to teach me, so it was an experimental discovery process that grew. It seemed like planting a seed and watching it grow, and what was happening in front of me felt magical. Cooking a dinner party for the local neighbours of sometimes 20 and even as many as 30 people at our open house for open mic and musical nights became the roots of my passion for cooking. I never used a recipe, just what I had on hand. From a young age, I was working school holidays in restaurants, and I often saw the cooks in action and imitated as best I could.

Sunday was our 'jamming night' and some people would bring a plate to share with everyone. The Unlisted Generator Band began a weekly gig held in our house, where we often squeezed large crowds into our little house, made up of four boxes and square cubes, placed alongside each other to make four rooms. Our bathroom was in the first box, the kitchen in the second box, then our living area in the third box, and the fourth box was our bedroom. There was an extra door, separating the toilet, from the large bathroom. Our bedroom was a

Music Night

quiet place where all the little kids were put down to sleep while we jammed into the early hours of Monday morning in the 70s. It took most of Monday to clean up the house on my own. I was lucky to have a normal loo, a flush toilet with a septic tank. The only one for miles, nearby neighbours had long drops, where everything was composted. When I visited my neighbours, going outside was at night was a frightening experience. The first time I heard a possum, sounded like a ghost.

We had a five-horsepower diesel generator called a Lister. It was an engine with a big flywheel that had to be crank started. It gave us electricity for a microphone, electric guitar, and organ/piano. We had many hand instruments, from bongo drums to shakers, even a wooden box with a stick and string stretched over it, making it an authentic hillbilly style, bass sound, plus many other instruments—I can remember one was called a Kazoo. This was our only form of entertainment in these early years. We had to bring back 44-gallon drums of diesel on a trailer. This was far too hard for me to do on my own. Using the generator was not daily as the cost of fuel wasn't worth it compared to driving the car around for six to seven hours.

These weekly gatherings stopped, as I was left with most of the cooking and cleaning for that many people, which took its toll on me. Sometimes in winter, we would have card nights with another family. It was things like this that made the long winter nights more fun. At one stage, we got a projector and showed movies onto a white bedsheet as our screen. This was to be the birthing of the 'film club'. Instead of dinner, we had supper, and herbal beverages, we roasted soya beans to grind to have healthy coffee. We tried our hand at wine-making and beer brewing.

Sometimes, I found catering to this many people, who didn't always contribute, far too much work for myself. The idea was to bring a plate to share yet often, some didn't bother and came empty-handed. Yet, when people contributed, we dined like kings and queens and played together harmoniously. "Those were the days my friends, I thought would never end" (Mary Hopkins 1968). It inspired me to cook with local ingredients, such as gathering mussels at low tide and collecting fresh duck and chicken eggs. We would take turns butchering a sheep to share in a radius of four to five miles for neighbours and the local community.

An Important thing to remember is that we didn't have refrigeration in the early days. In later years, I acquired a kerosene fridge because the fresh milk would not keep for a day in the summer. This was raw and un-pasteurised milk. Interesting that city kids' concept of milk was that it's delivered to their front door in glass bottles. Few realised it was taken from a cow, which can only produce milk after giving birth.

Music Night

In those days, we could buy a whole side of lamb from the local butcher for $25. Now, it costs more than that for one forequarter leg. I researched that a side can vary in price from $150 to over $250 depending on the weight. There's a saying that hard work makes us stronger. I believe this was my reality. What doesn't kill you, will make you stronger. I honestly thought all this hard work built resilience through perseverance, giving me physical and emotional strength, and helping me achieve life's challenges.

Even now, whenever we might have a storm or electricity black out, I always have matches and candles around.

BETWEEN TWO WORLDS

My take on between two worlds is from different angles: First, from the perspective of being torn between my love for two countries and second, my inner and outer world.

I was born in Hong Kong decades ago when it was still British-governed. Then, I was six years old in 1960 when my family immigrated to New Zealand. I was too young to remember Hong Kong as it was then and have never felt any connection on my return visits as an adult to feel any sense of home. Although I went looking, I never felt any resonations. Growing up in New Zealand made it my home country. The big brother, Australia and the little sister, New Zealand.

When I read the book *Wild Swans: Three Daughters of China* it shocked me at how the Chinese treated their own! I became despondent and had trouble resonating with or accepting it as my culture. I have often called myself a banana: yellow on the outside and white on the inside. Growing up, I didn't see myself as Chinese first, and in my 30s, I preferred to call myself a citizen of the universe.

I realise we are not our past; this is often how I feel as my situation changes, and I need to adapt to those changes.

I felt very bonded growing up in New Zealand and right at home there. New Zealand is my homeland, not China. As I said before, I was born in Hong Kong while it was under British rule, but I was not entitled to a British passport. We travelled with Hong Kong ones that we surrendered on becoming naturalized New Zealanders. I refuse to say I was born in China; I say I was born in Hong Kong when it was still under British rule, as I feel it is my personal political statement. I don't agree with China's policies, especially in how they treat their own people and the lack of freedom of speech. The government lacks respect for Chinese people and the other nationalities that live there. They are called Hong Kongers or Hong Kongonese. Even being born there, I don't fit, nor qualify.

As of 1st July 1997, sovereignty over the British Colony of Hong Kong was transferred to China. The handover raised questions about the capacity of the territory to continue its economic success and maintain the political freedoms and the rule of law enjoyed under British rule.

My last visit during a stopover on my then annual trip to the UK was affected by large demonstrations, mainly by students rebelling. They didn't want to lose their freedom of speech. I experienced heavy security to proof of travel before I was even allowed back inside the airport after my brief stopover.

I continue to identify with the Indigenous Māori culture, embracing it as my own, so much more than China, a place where it would be impossible for me to feel that same sense of home. I visited twice, and both times, I felt like a stranger in a strange land.

Having lived most of my life in New Zealand, I have travelled widely and have become a citizen of the universe. In an interview with a local paper for a solo exhibition of my artworks, the reporter used the term, "I am a citizen of the universe," and I felt it fit me well, so I've since adopted this term. I'm not attaching myself to being of one nation; thus, the labelling of being a citizen of the universe resonates well. I love learning about and experiencing different cultures. I have adopted ways of being open to new experiences and tasting food from all over the world through my travels.

My soul became universal; I followed a chubby Indian guru younger than myself from a Christian Anglican upbringing. I fell in love with a handsome white hippie and ran away from home to a bush farm some 30 miles from the nearest town. I was a vegetarian before, who learnt to kill my own meat and grow my own vegetables, which was a necessity. Being sustainable and living off the land was a conscious choice. Chickens were the only animals I killed myself, anything bigger was the man's job. Just my fun figure of speech. And my man loved his meat. He didn't feel satisfied with a vegetarian diet all the time. I brought up two children without electricity. I milked five cows daily, made my own cheese, and ground wheat into flour to make my bread in a camp oven over the open fire. I not only cooked everything from scratch but learnt to improvise with what ingredients I had on hand to feed my family.

Along with growing my own vegetables, I occasionally collected mussels for protein at low tide on the local beach. No refrigeration meant limited protein, so we took turns with others within a six-to-ten-mile range to slaughter a sheep and share it around. Free-range hens for eggs, and when we had extra eggs, we traded them for local honey. It was a hard life filled with the adventure of learning new skills for survival. It truly was an incredible and exciting adventure at the young age of 20.

I say this next thing with humour: at one stage, I was the county's first lady as Roger became the county chairman and a local politician. I was invited to speak at the local Lions Club, when I returned from a visit to China and Hong Kong, to share my travel experiences.

Being virtually the only Chinese person in the area, I was requested to teach Chinese cooking with evening and weekend classes in the local town of Westport. I had never taught at all, let alone a 'how to cook' type class. I was cooking each dish as I went along, trying out the dishes only a few weeks before each class to determine the quantity of each ingredient, rather than throwing in what I felt, as I love to do freely when I cook at home. I had to measure each ingredient and write a recipe that could be printed for the students to take home. So, I decided to give it a go with a fake it 'til you make it attitude. I made up each recipe as I went along, even starting a small catering business where I had my daughters help me wrap wonton dumplings for me when I catered for dinner parties in the West Coast region of the South Island of New Zealand. I didn't realise how much of an entrepreneur I was at the time. There's a saying that if you do something 10,000 times, you become a natural at doing it and owning it. The more I did it, the easier it became.

My grandmother, whom I vividly remember passed away when I was only three years old, taught me to 'pound her bones,' the traditional style of Chinese massage. I'm grateful for the skill I inherited because Roger became a shearer. Shearing was his main job on the West Coast in the early days, providing an income to feed our family, and it was very hard on his back with all the bending, so I began to massage him. I attended training with local therapists. I learnt from each of them and years later, massaging became a career. I got qualifications for it and made a great living out of it for a long time. Without that income, I would never qualified for a loan to buy my first house.

When Roger's back pain first started flaring up, I started drawing on my PawPaw's (name for maternal grandmother) teaching and developed my healing massage style. I incorporated techniques from attending courses of different modalities and learnt the difference between a chiropractor and a naturopath. I got my family's iris eye readings (Iridologist) to access the state of our health from the reading of our eyes.

My daughters called my mother PawPaw, and when they had their children, I became PawPaw to the boys. My two girls each had a boy. I have also seen it written as PorPor. A father's mother is called Maa-Maa. Each grandma is given a name that identifies each connection and hard learning and understanding, then an actual name pinpoints the relative's position, like first cousin on the paternal or maternal. Clearly identifying the connection on side of mother or father.

During the later years of my relationship with Roger, I began feeling lost. I later realised that I was never allowed to say what I wanted to. I didn't even see it as controlling until years later when I attended self-development classes.

Being a homemaker without electricity was no easy task. Despite being a hippie, Roger had some old-school values. If he was out earning money, he didn't feel a need to lift a finger with any housekeeping at home and this eventually led to our relationship breakdown. He dressed and acted like a hippie, but his thoughts were of old fashion male chauvinism, which, for me, was like a dagger separating our love. I remember asking him if we could have relationship counselling. He commented that it was my problem and that I should sort it out myself as it was not his concern. Those were the sorts of words and comments that made me feel depressed when I started to become more aware that I didn't have a voice in life. It wasn't until years later that I realised it was the lack of respect that drove me away. If he had heard and met me halfway, we would have and could have had more time together, but it seemed our relationship had passed its " use-by" date.

The hard work of keeping the home fires burning without support and being not respected broke me. I felt I had lost myself. I didn't know who I was, and I wasn't the same carefree-spirited young girl I was before I fell in love. Roger felt if he was working, then I had to keep the home fires burning. Not everyone knows how or understands the level of difficulties involved in living off the grid until they have actually experienced it for themselves. Like what it took to keep a wood and coal range going 24/7. The coal range heated up a copper water cylinder giving us hot water on tap and heated the home in winter. If the chimney wasn't kept and cleaned on a regular basis, or the batch of coal wasn't good quality, it was a major drawback in more ways than one. Black specks would be blown into the room upon opening the fire door, creating extra housework. It was a hard skill to learn the best way to use the coal range to get the best performance from it. The new electric versions of these old classic ranges are around $15,000. In the 1980s, we put in a remodelled version for $1000, how's that for a comparison?

Roger often rushed out to work, leaving me without dry firewood. I had to think on my feet with two small kids, so I often tied up string or bailing twine over the living room to dry clothes and nappies. He complained it was like coming home to a Chinese laundromat but took no responsibility for his part in our situation. He only had to learn to cook and do his own washing after I left. My daughter told me on a trip home from boarding school that she had to iron a huge pile of business shirts for him because when he was busy, it was much easier to just buy a new shirt.

His father was the breadwinner, and his mother had everything super organised. But as I'm writing, I realise she was so efficient because she didn't start as young as I did and had electricity on tap. I often even felt a bit judged by her because she had this attitude during her visits, like I should be jumping up to wait on Roger as soon as he walked in as she did for her husband. A different time, a different era, yet I felt I could speak the same language with her. I learnt so much from Roger's mum, Pam. We communicated but didn't always agree. Still, I felt closer to her. My mother spoke very little English, I spoke very little Cantonese. So, inspite of our differences Pam and I bonded over our shared love for Roger and the girls. She gave the grandchildren and great-grandchildren permission to call her Pam. My own mother couldn't understand this, thinking it was disrespectful, but it was what Pam requested.

I stayed on the farm until the children were older; my eldest was at boarding school and the younger was 11. I returned to my home city to live with my mother in Wellington, the capital city of New Zealand, with a population that's equal only to Melbourne.

I lost myself in bringing up my children in a lifestyle I embraced to love that was not my own choice. But it was that way of living that gave me so much strength. I arrived as a naïve, young girl and came out as a strong-willed woman in the 18 years I was there. I was 20 when I arrived on the farm and gave birth a couple of months before I turned 21. I didn't know how much hard work was involved in living on the land or raising children. I learnt the hard way. And it was after nearly 18 years I felt I needed to find myself again. We did try continuing with a long-distance relationship of some sort; however, communication was a huge issue. I understood myself at the end of our relationship, so I knew I had to leave to find myself, again.

During our time apart, he would make me cassette tapes of a composition of songs titled: *Stand by Your Man, Love Is All You Need, We Can Work It Out*. There were many more, but after all these years, I can only recall a few. I guess a male thinks differently, whereas I rather have a deeper form of communication, such as talking it out. He seemed to be in a fantasy land that he was trying to connect via music, but to me, he wasn't seeing the situation or what I was feeling, he only saw it from his own personal perspective. With compromise, I considered relocating to Nelson where our eldest daughter went to boarding school. It was three hours' drive from the farm, named on the map as Pahautane.

I started reading the book, *The 5 Languages of Love*, which discusses how each person speaks their own love language. Louise Hay's book became my bible, and "You Can Heal Your Life," was my motto. My friends asked me why I was leaving after taking so many years to finally get electricity and acquire all the mod cons like a dishwasher. It sounded great, but material things were unimportant after so many years of struggling. Why couldn't I just stay and enjoy it? By then, I'd had enough of feeling enslaved to the home, like I had lost my sense of freedom and spirit. I needed to do some soul-searching in reverse compared to those who escaped the city to live on the land. I had to go back to the city to find myself.

So, in my mid-30s, I chose to return to the city where I grew up to redefine who I was and who I had become after so many challenges from the hard lifestyle and often wet and rainy weather conditions.

When I ran away from my family home at 20 with near zero work history other than waitressing in my family restaurant in central Wellington, I had very little confidence. So, I reinvented myself on my return. When I returned to Wellington, I found work in a central city massage centre, up Plimmer Steps, a prominent landmark in the CBD area of the city. The building was sub-letting a space for a massage business, where we had to build our own clients or just take walk-ins. There were two male owners before me, who each had a different way of management. When I took over, I did it my way.

Starting with only working a half-day a week, I quickly learnt to manage the business before taking it over and within three years, I bought the business. To this day, I still don't know how I did it; I had no fundamental strategies or business skills, but with a deep sense of feeling in my heart, it felt right.

I did all this from my heart, which guided my head. I didn't know how to run a business, but my clientele grew through a combination of my intuition and skills. I often had people waiting on return visits to see me and they had to book up to two weeks in advance or try a new therapist with less experience for the same rates, which was $25 for half an hour and $40 for an hour. My skills were in demand. I learnt how to listen to my client's needs on a deeper level, beyond just working on the surface. I developed unique techniques that catered to everyone. During this period, I attended workshops and continued taking more classes, even incorporating another modality called kinesiology. I read books like *The Hands of Light* and worked with a Reiki form of energy. I joined many groups to expand and understand the levels of the healing process.

I was a certified and registered member of MINZ (Massage Institute of New Zealand)

When I retired, the rates were $35 for half an hour and $60 for an hour. I incorporated 90-minute sessions that I felt were the most beneficial for $75. I went to a holistic therapist who flew down from Auckland every, month for a week in an apartment she owned and did her healing work from. She worked on energy, like a technique called Reiki, above the body with hardly any physical touch with fees of close to $300. Sessions of at least an hour and a half and up to three hours. I went many times, and she was also in high demand. I had a policy that after every 10 hours of my giving in my work, I would receive an hour of some other form of therapy. After treatment, of energy work, I often felt like I was floating, a memorable, unforgettable experience.

Within six years, I bought a house. And without realising just how, the universe guided me to what became a home and income, house-owner. I was lucky to be shown this house a day before it went on the market. It was nothing like what I had in mind, far from it. It was an older-style wooden house, with two bedrooms on the ground floor and two on the upper floor with separate entrances. I lived in the upstairs flat rent-free while renting out the bottom to cover my mortgage. Not a calculated business plan at all. This just fell on my lap. It was the law of attraction in action.

At the time, I had no idea just how intelligent and wise my decision was or maybe it was a stroke of good luck. In a massive way, the universe was telling me I made the right choice to leave the farm where I probably would have never had the opportunity to draw on this inner source of wisdom.

I remember when I was shown the house late in the afternoon, the lighting was poor, and all I could smell was the lingering smell of curry. I didn't like it, and it wasn't what I was looking for, but something in my gut said I must take it. This was a private viewing the night before it was officially advertised. I realised years later, upon reflection on what happened, that this was another gift from the universe.

During seven years of long hours, massaging seven to nine hours a day and sometimes up to six days a week, I gradually built on my confidence and self-esteem. It was after this (maybe it was that seven-year itch that burnt me out; possibly from the loss of passion, as well) that I developed repetitive strain injury (RSI) in my arms. I had trouble holding a mug without pain. I believe it was the universe's sign telling me to move on.

So, I retired from the business and went travelling, and being an adventurer following my heart, I planned a seven-country trip. I intended to sub-lease the business, which was difficult, so I ended up selling the business for a low price to a therapist who turned it into a second business placing his new students to work there. It was time to let go and move on, which was precisely what I did. With my passion slowly fading, I knew I needed to take a break. Back then, I thought I might return to start another business, which didn't happen. I put it down to not be able to go backwards and to go forwards instead. Learn from the experience of the lesson.

Onto the next journey, I stepped into the shoes I was destined to wear. I wandered around the world for four months, with the first leg beginning in Australia for a couple of weeks, first in Sydney seeing old friends, then onto Byron Bay where I was drawn to visit Crystal Castle before flying to Athens, Greece. There, I backpacked around the Islands of Greece with no set plans; I followed my nose around Europe solo. It was an incredibly empowering journey. I hopped on a ferry from Greece to Italy, then Eurostar's fast train to Holland and Demark. From there, I flew over to the United Kingdom. One thing I particularly remembered, was speaking English using what I call improvised pidgin English, which was English and a bit of Greek. In England, I could speak without having to find translations from my little book of phrases.

The time I spent in London during the cooler months, catching up with old friends and even making new ones, was a big contrast from the summer I spent in Greece. One thing I loved about being in the UK was travelling on the double-decker buses around the properties from the original Monopoly board game. While in the USA, I took Greyhound buses everywhere, with the highlights being Disneyland in Los Angeles. I was also very impressed by Las Vegas, and I visited the most magnificent bookstore in Portland that extended two blocks. By the time my trip to the USA ended, I was so worn out from such exciting travels that I decided to skip Canada and return home to Wellington, New Zealand.

During my trip, I started journaling and writing recipes for the cookbook I originally wanted to write.

Now, what's next? The start of a new story in my life…

On my return, I felt a little lost again, wondering what to do workwise. I had a few private massage clients that kept in touch, so I did some massage work at my home and did some massage callouts with my portable massage table to earn a bit of pocket money. I knew in my gut going back to professional massage was over. I did my time—seven years—and it was time for a change.

I took advantage of the government's re-skilling training courses. Having always been interested in fashion and art, I decided on silk screen printing for six months, designing and hand printing t-shirts for events with the Bowerman School of Design. I even designed and made a head tablecloth out of a big white bed sheet, which I hand-dyed, to a sea blue, turquoise, teal, that I printed giant seashells onto it, with a reddish-brown henna. This was for a friend's wedding held on the beach at Rarotonga.

With just under a year of fashion design experience, I took on a few private jobs designing logos for martial arts studios and sports clubs, plus outfits for a couple of musical bands. Finding I had time to indulge in making art, I explored my creative side.

I had a friend in charge of planning exhibitions at the Wellington Museum called Te Papa, who told me there was a Gianni Versace collection about to tour in my hometown. So, I liaised a deal for the school with my friend from April to July 2001. We had fun being able to draft a few patterns and express our love of fashion, and just chatted—we even got paid for this. It was a fantastic few months of fun.

I instigated this exhibition at Te Papa (Wellington Museum) for the design school; I helped put this school on the map, at the time, so to speak, and I even put this on my CV. The sewing teacher asked if I didn't feel I needed permission from the owner of the school, but I don't remember if I bothered. This is my story, and I tell it as I experienced it. This exhibition of Versace garments came to Wellington before touring the rest of the world.

That's why sometimes, it's not what you know, but who you know. I put the idea of using students and the school in the exhibit, showing drafting, and sewing skills; this was another brain wave that I, in a way, manifested. Being involved in a museum exhibition was terrific, as it was my dream to be a tour guide, and I half fulfilled this dream.

I Googled it, but there's nothing on the home page regarding the input of the school participating, but I know it was because I contacted my fellow students to confirm dates. That friend, Polly Filla, a top drag queen of Wellington moved to Melbourne a bit before I did. Her fabulous lip-sync and ability to groove in those kinky high heels made her act stand out from all the rest. I don't know how many drag artists can design and sew up such outrageously stunning costumes, but it is one of the special talents she developed, a skill that grew from thousands of hours of practice. Watching her Facebook gigs was a highlight that made me laugh during lockdown (COVID-19). I enjoyed saying I went to school with her alias as Colin, some people wondered because I was around the age of his mother. This was the chapter of my life as an adult student.

Once again, I was wondering what my next step would be.

FROM NO JOB TO TWO JOBS

After years of court battles and the passing of my mother, I was very depressed and unable to work. I found a little inspiration from Steve Jobs and my own determination when I passed the second step in becoming a 'trolly dolly', which used to be another name for an air hostess (my dream job as a teenager). Then I found out the first 18 months would be on domestic flights with long shifts, four days on, three days off, and sometimes stayovers in another city overnight. Even some likelihood of the occasional 18-hour day. This was something that didn't thrill me.

Then out of the blue, a friend told me to have a look into bus driving, saying it paid more, and I would be able to sleep in my own bed. The training was free, including the cost of my heavy trade licence. So, I took up bus driving. I wanted to own a house truck or bus as I was captured by the possibility of doing a *Priscilla Queen of the Desert* adventure, driving a mobile home. Touring around Australia was a bit of a daydream, that never eventuated.

It felt amazing and empowering driving a bus, I loved it, and I could choose my shifts with hours that suited my lifestyle. Since returning to the city, I found a community art studio where I could play and explore my creativity with art.

My friend from Vincent's Art Workshop worked as a cook at a childcare centre needed to go away and wanted me to hold her job open for her return.

The day started with a pickup in a taxi at 5 am to be taken to the bus depot in Karori. I drove the first bus out of the depot and started picking up passengers and dropping them into the city. Then I worked as a school bus driver picking up students, taking them to Rongotai college. I returned the bus to the Kilbirnie depot at 9.30am. From there, I would bus into the city where I was the lunch cook for an inner-city childcare day centre.

I got to plan the menus and create a shopping list. All the ingredients I needed were delivered and I had a budget to stick to. As I loved kids, I loved doing this job. Using some old menus and guidelines made the job a breeze. I would start by putting out morning tea for around 30 children, then start on lunch. Lunch would be served at 11:30 am, clean-up done by 12:30 pm, and afternoon tea would be laid out and covered, so I was out of there by 1.30 pm. From there, I bused into the CBD and did some art at Vincent's Art Workshop for a few hours, then headed home again. Not having to drive my car and find parking in the city was such a bonus. I even got a free bus pass for my partner at the time; how cool is that?

I was able to do both jobs by juggling and planning my time wisely. With bus driving, I took on the earliest shift starting with a 5 am pickup in a taxi outside my front door. I got a free bus pass, which meant when I finished my shift at 9 am I could travel into the city in my bus driver's uniform, so I didn't even need to show my bus pass. This meant I could be at the childcare centre at 9.30 am, perfect timing.

I loved working in a childcare centre during this time, and I became a bus driver as my ex never allowed me to drive him—something I've found to be quite familiar with some men, as often, men prefer to drive instead of being driven…especially back around this time. So, this was proving to myself and him that I could do anything I wanted. Despite this being over 10 years after I left him, I got an invite to his wedding.

My Australian driver's licence still carries the heavy trade endorsement, which was on my New Zealand, licence on arrival here, but it must be renewed at a high cost every three years. Interestingly, in Australia, it just stays on forever. What a contrast.

As dreams and goals are just stepping stones along the way, we explore possible options that can often branch into directions we would have never dreamt of as a possibility at all in the beginning. Life just keeps unfolding, much like chapters in a book.

After a couple of years, I wanted to explore art and creativity, so I gave up both jobs to become a full-time art student. I discovered myself to be a bit of an artist and had a string of successful exhibitions—in groups and with solo shows, some becoming sold-out events. I was crazy enough to turn them into musical soirees, inviting promising young musicians to play to promote their talents. Those were exciting and fun times.

HAPPY BIRTHDAY

I had an invitation to attend the 80th birthday party for Mary Helen my 'Fairy God Mother' in March 2008 in Melbourne, which opened my eyes to yet another chapter of adventure. At this party, the performer was God-like tanned, almost naked. A young stud lap dancer performing a private lap dance with over 40 pairs of eyes on her, and her "Private Dancer" enjoying watching her pleasure just as much as the performer—what a blast of fun and laughter; it was the catalyst to my new chapter in life.

At her party, there were six or seven singers who were part of the 'Choir of Hard Knocks' performing and leading the singalong as part of the entertainment. This happened because her daughter, Martina who lived in Paris, would come to Melbourne to stay with her brother, so we sort of became odd sisters, not connected by blood. She volunteered with the choir of Hard Knocks. I even stayed with her in Paris for a few days back in 1998, something I only connected during the editing of my stories. I was so impressed by them and their singing that I went to their weekly rehearsal the following Monday morning after seeing them on Friday and I signed up to be a member. This small holiday of four weeks totally transformed my future. With that, I acknowledge Martina's part of organising her mother's 80th birthday. This led me to see the Choir of Hard Knocks, which lead me to make such a quick decision, without any hesitation to shift countries, such a quick impulsive decision without doubt, and with so much clarity. No regrets.

It took me more than two trips back and forth between Australia and New Zealand to empty everything in my big house; what belongings I didn't sell were given to friends, with the bulk going to charity. I cleaned out my fully furnished two-story, three-bedroom house with a double garage.

As I still had some scheduled tutoring classes throughout that year, I flew back to honour my commitment.

Even though I got rid of many items, I spent a fair bit of money putting some memorabilia into storage for years. This was a waste as I eventually gave so much away again over time. More sorting on each visit, almost 10 years of paid storage costing thousands of dollars, letting go of material with emotional attachment felt like taking vitamins on slow release.

HAPPY BIRTHDAY

On reflection now, it seemed pointless paying so much to store things I didn't need. I have far less now, but I still own too many *material* things. For example, clothing I don't wear and books I collect but never read. Kitchen gadgets, now that's another story.

There was an accumulation of stuff in storage as I travelled, and when I went back to support my daughter about 11 years ago, I took everything I owned to storage here in Maribyrnong (Melbourne) when I went to Hong Kong, my birth country. I thought some new opportunities would keep me there, but that wasn't in my destiny. It did mean did mean that once I decided it was better to rent my own place. I had almost everything I needed to furnish my new home already in storage. A bonus I prepared for without realising.

I felt an incredible sense of freedom getting rid of unnecessary things and only keeping some family items of meaning with my belongings in New Zealand. There was no value in all the things in storage and I ended up paying so much money to keep up storage both in New Zealand and Australia that, in time, it became much less important and easier to let it all go. Settling down in my own place in Melbourne's West, reduced the adventures. But I still visited family in the United Kingdom and New Zealand.

I believe that letting go of things takes steps and time, which varies from person to person. The process of self-awareness happens differently for each person, and I'm sharing my own story, as each individual has their own personal discovery.

Moving countries is like having two lovers. I divide myself between the countries. Do I want to be here, or do I want to be there? It was a real dilemma and conflict that took a couple of years to become clear.

Melbourne is the bigger version of Wellington. It's a café city, like Melbourne, with many similar familiarities. Interesting fact: the entire population of New Zealand is the same as the population of just Melbourne. Yet, the cultural diversity is far greater in Melbourne. The museums and art galleries completely blew me away. And another fun fact I enjoy sharing: there are far more sheep than people in New Zealand.

I started volunteering for Lentil As Anything which was a pay-as-you-can-afford restaurant—people paid what they could afford into a donating box towards the meal. In a short amount of time, I became a branch manager and was also cooking and floor managing as well for a year, five to six days a week, before wearing myself out again—history and patterns of my life that I started to become aware of, even more so after writing and editing my stories. Within weeks, I became a paid/

chef cook, as it was not classiflied as a tax deductible job as such, I had super fast promotions. Floor manger to restaurant manager with a space of few weeks.

Unheard of at the time, as one young man, had to volunteer around a year to raise from volunteering (unpaid) to a paid floor manager. I woke up each morning early with excitement and passion for the day, I walked into Footscray from West Footscray in the darkness around 6 am to get there for my 8 am start. I remember the quietness, lighting the gas commercial ovens. Starting early gave me quiet time by myself to plan that day's menu with what was there in the cool store walk-in fridge. I had to juggle my day off on Mondays to keep on singing with the choir.

On the anniversary of the choir's 10th birthday, we sang a national tour of Perth, Uluru, and Sydney. The main highlight being placed at the centre of the stage… Being placed at the centre of the stage singing in the Sydney Opera House. We were so lucky Jetstar sponsored all our flights. It was a thrilling experience at our Adelaide concert, where Maggie Beer was our MC. I shared a hug with her after our performance, and this big bear hug from her made it such a significant highlight for me.

Between my two worlds, two countries, some 14 years on, we just celebrated the 15th birthday of the Choir of Hard Knocks in September 2021. I moved here roughly half a year after the choir started, therefore, at each choir birthday, I would have been here six months less. The choir was founded by Dr Jonathan Welsh. I'm still loving my singing and no longer feel torn. I'm happy to be at home where I feel that sense of belonging. The choir became my family.

Even as I write this, singing creates happy vibrations, a natural, drug-free happy hit during these 18 months of lockdowns. I have learnt to fly with singing rehearsals, Zumba dance classes, exercise classes, and meditation circles all on Zoom.

Zoom has become the new flying for those of us still in lockdown. I even experienced a Zoom walking tour of Venice. I have joined writing groups held at different branches of the local libraries, that continued on Zoom during lockdown. It's my new way of travelling while sitting safely in the comfort of my living room. It takes me here and there on virtual journeys around the world and between my worlds of New Zealand and Australia.

IN THE BEGINNING

My family immigrated from Hong Kong to New Zealand in the 1960s. It was my parents and us three kids who were sponsored by the Anglican church. It took six weeks on an ocean liner, stopping briefly in Sydney, Australia. I remember that none of us spoke a word of English.

Onboard, there was a Chinese and an English dining room. Often, people were too seasick to get up for breakfast, so we three kids would have breakfast in both the dining rooms. I am sure this is the time I gained my sea legs.

I vaguely remember seeing little black specks of soot on the crisp white sheet in our family room and climbing up on a bed to peer out the porthole window, which must have been open some of the time for the air to circulate. The dark specks on the beds were due to the pollution from the streamliner coming in the open window.

These were my earliest memories of having a sense of adventure. My siblings and I had fun in our temporary home. We wandered around the ship unsupervised, watching people, foreign people, speaking languages that were strange to our ears. The only language I knew at this age was Cantonese and little did I know, until I was an adult, that this wasn't the only language spoken by Chinese people.

The first English words I remember ever saying was, "Sorry monkey." Then I added on these words in Cantonese, "Tai tol chi," which translated to, "Big tummy button." "Sorry Monkey, big tummy button," makes no sense but it's a memory I treasure from that age because it was when I began being aware of adventure. I don't know how or where we picked up these words we just repeated them, like a song, as we thought it was funny at the time.

On board the ship, we watched people play croquet and shoot discs across marked squares on the wooden deck. Such a carefree experience and the root foundations of my journeys of adventures yet to come.

The highlight of the voyage was when we crossed the equator, possibly the fondest memory of this massive journey of six weeks on an ocean liner. The crew put on a show—the re-enactment of King Neptune. The storyline I never understood as a child, but I will never forget the fun of that experience. There were no spoken lines, just a mime, that had the audience roaring in laughter.

As an adult, I have researched this and found it was typical of most liners to put on some sort of play or show while crossing the equator, and some liners even issued a certificate to passengers for crossing the equator. I can specifically remember in the show there was King Neptune who had his tummy cut open and a string of sausages pulled out, and with my research, I also found that each liner and set of crews dramatized the story in their own way. Something I intend to do more research on in the future is to find more traces and actual documentation of the ship my family immigrated on.

On arrival, we knew no one and were met, literally 'fresh off the boat' by the Reverend of the Anglican Church that sponsored us. The minister gave my siblings and me English names so we would fit in at school. I remember he was a kind and caring man, who invited our family to have meals with his family, wife, and three children. Having no close family growing up, they embraced us into their family and into the flock of their church and faith.

Once we got television, I started watching TV shows about different families, and I joined groups which gave me that sense of family. I enjoyed watching a British series called *Fair Exchange*, where two teenage girls were swapped from England and the USA. These TV shows gave me a perspective of what a happy family looked like. Real or not, they seemed to be happy families. Watching their interactions with their siblings, parents, and grandparents gave me that sense of what a happy family was all about, or so I thought.

These days, as I write this part of my life, my family isn't in the same country I choose to live in. My immediate family is my two girls. I see my daughter and grandson in the UK once every 18 months or so. I have had two trips in a short space of a couple of months…at least I did before the COVID-19 pandemic. I was pursuing an opportunity, with coaches, to develop a business that never eventuated, but it gave me that sense of belonging.

Last time, on my first night with my daughter in London, after a few hours, we seemed to pick up where we left off when we last saw each other. We forgot all time and distance and it didn't take long to feel as though we had not been apart.

Each time I leave for home after my stay in the UK, I feel as if I leave a part of me behind, often feeling a bit lost, the first week or so. And after each trip, as I've aged, it seems to take more time than normal for me to settle. Adjusting to the time difference can take 36 to 40-something hours depending on the route and the airline. This is known as a long-haul trip, with at least

IN THE BEGINNING

one stop but often even more. So, it's important to weigh up all this before booking.

I can imagine that every mother or grandmother who doesn't live in the same country as her children and grandchildren would likely identify with these feelings of missing them from a far. Distance can make the heart fonder, missing family and friends who live far away.

MY PAWPAW

This story is about my pawpaw (Cantonese for maternal grandmother) and some of the memories I have of her.

She told me that when you cook with love, love always transfers into the food. Therefore, I always say when food is cooked with love, no matter what you are cooking, this food is always life-giving. There's a saying I have taken on board: you become what you eat. I'm not as pure with my eating as I would like to be. I can often overeat and eat food that may not be super bad for me but borders on being naughty. Eating food that's cooked with love and care is always far more enjoyable for me than eating takeaways.

When I cook, I often cook according to my mood and feelings, using whatever ingredients I have on hand.

My grandma just loved to cook for her family, even when we said we weren't hungry. Sometimes, the aroma of her cooking made me salivate and occasionally, certain smells turned on the tap to my food-loving memories. It may not even be a scent anyone else can smell in the air coming from my memory bank. A scent from food can trigger all sorts of memories.

I would like to say when I cook, I prefer not to follow a recipe. I get inspired to use the ingredients I have available at the time to invent and create from my intuition, just as I watched my grandma do. At the age of three, I would sit on a stool, mesmerised from watching her in action concocting tasty dishes that not only fed the body but the soul as well. Food created from the heart has a unique homemade element that isn't often found in eating out. Eating out often doesn't resonate with me the same way it used to. Maybe it was due to so much time in lockdown and my taste being sensitive to food enhancers as well.

When eating out, even in a very expensive restaurant, it's almost impossible for me to have the same earthiness as I get from a dish created from scratch. I used to love eating out as I've always enjoyed tasting new things I haven't been exposed to. But I'm more sensitive now, so my love for eating out has lost its appeal.

Pawpaw made a fried egg in a wok that she called a 'pocket purse egg', put on top of a piping hot bowl of fluffy

MY PAWPAW

white rice with a light drizzle of soy. It felt like heaven, remembering such strong memories of her cooking. I've made it for myself thousands of times and as I eat it, I'm reminded of the loving touch my grandma infused them with. I cook it in her honour.

NEW COMPUTER: MY NEW LIFE TO BECOME A WRITER

I'm journal writing, as a way a way to practice my writing every day. Like everything, what I write isn't just about my book, it's a record of my thoughts and feelings. Sometimes I refer to many names when talking about my laptop, my computer, and even my typewriter; what's in a name when they all mean the same thing? I am hitting this device (I'm calling it a typewriter now) with two fingers, not using the full scale of all my fingers, as I have not learnt to touch type.

I have named every car I have ever owned, just for the fun of it, rather than just calling it *my car*. Example: Betty-Blue, Silver-Chariot, Woman in Red, Electric Green Bubble, Blue Lagoon, and Yellow Submarine, which was an off-mustard colour. The latter had no power steering and was very heavy to drive. I had to get it checked out by a family friend who was a mechanic. The mechanical side was sound, I had no idea that the stiffness, or difficulty, was to change gears. I had so much pain I wondered if I was having a heart attack, I had to figure out the cause, and once I realised, it was a relief.

There were a few more, even one that I was silly enough to bid for at the car auctions that I never checked. Bidding wildly after I missed out on the ones I had previously checked out before the auction started. Buying a car without inspection, just because I liked the colour, I must admit is one of the silliest choices I've ever made. It even had to be pushed off the bidding lot because of the terrible state it was in. I ended up reselling it at a big loss. It was an impulsive decision, lessons that are costly on different levels, has helped me see the patterns.

I must admit, typing is much easier than handwriting, especially given there is less pressure than holding a pen to paper. Another thing I particularly enjoy is never having to carry and keep track of so many little bits and pieces of paper that can either get wet or lost; I just make sure the carry case keeps my laptop protected from any form of damage. I would often get sudden ideas and instead of writing them, it was faster and easier to open my little laptop as I was often travelling, either on a plane or bus. Taking breaks to glance at the scenery.

NEW COMPUTER: MY NEW LIFE TO BECOME A WRITER

I chose a red device because red is my favourite colour, and it stands out! It's interesting how the colour red features so much in my life. In reference to an old pop song, I listened to when I was growing up, *Black is Black* by Los Bravos. It was an old song I used to sing to myself. My version is *Red is Red, I want to type it all down.* As I love singing and music, I write in a particular style that points out similarities of creativity in my stories. With splashes of humour that highlight using literary metaphors and hopefully, without getting into too long of an explanation. I often break out into song, doing my own expression of *Glee*, a TV music series. I have come to realise that this is the essence of who I am, as I have read, and re-read the words that I have written, I have begun to know more about myself, and even in some ways, how repetitive some of my experiences are. I am unfolding a deeper understanding, more of who I am.

Yes, to no more bits of paper and afterwards trying to collate them, but in the past, when inspiration came, I grabbed whatever I could write on, like the back of my travel itinerary. From now on, this device, my laptop, will become my treasure chest, as it holds my greatest treasures. My words, the stories I have inside me, that need to come out, that need to be shared. Here, everything I write will be stored in my little red treasure chest and my little red laptop will become my constant companion, lying beside me in bed, ready to input and share my thoughts and feelings, to be able to continue my passion to write. After this, I invested and upgraded to an expensive phone with a stylus pen to write directly onto my phone and record my stories. I'm gradually growing my technical awareness of modern devices.

I often dress in all red as well. When I was typing at the local library close to where I was house sitting, on a trip to my old hometown, a woman came up and said how much I stood out wearing all different shades of red and typing on a red laptop. This brought more awareness that I hadn't thought about previously, she even asked if I would or could house sit for her in the future.

RECONNECTING WITH A LONG, FORGOTTEN FRIEND

I have just made a major realisation that everything I write seems to be about how I see the situation or the world. I need to explore other mediums and genres, explore non-fiction to fiction, find the spellcheck function in Word and get more familiar with it.

It's been awesome reconnecting with my old friend, Janjo. I have asked permission to use her name as it's such a lovely and unusual name. It's been 12 years or so, and it's nice to pick up where we left off. I hadn't realised how young she was back then. It was such an honour to see a framed photo of us on her wall from some 12 or 13 years before. She's 39 now, which is a few months younger even than my youngest daughter. I had no idea just how young she was when we met, and I totally forgot that I gave her a piece of my artwork from an exhibition in the studio below the radio station. I must remember to take a picture of that too. As a university student, she was a volunteer technician for the live-access radio shows I did for close to eight years. Pre-recording if I was too busy on the day to do the show live.

The framed photo of us taken at a themed party together was a forgotten memory that resurfaced after seeing it. It was a white party, and I went over the top by dressing as a bride, carrying a white artificial flower bouquet. I remember having white roller shoes with red trim. I remember having difficulty roller-walking as I couldn't really skate, so I had to hold onto the walls and other people. This made it even more fun and enjoyable. Putting in the effort, even me by dressing up. Creating an atmosphere that fits with the theme is important. These memories would not have surfaced if Janjo and I had not reconnected last year to make such a fruitful connection. I used to love themed parties as I enjoyed dressing up. I called it getting into the zone and would often win the best-dressed prize of a bottle of wine or a bar tab. It was a lovely reward for going to the effort, all in aid of expressing the essence of fun!

Any time there was a Halloween party, I used stage make-up. I would whiten my face, put on plastic fangs, paint a bit of fake blood on my chin, and even don a black Dracula cape. Another time, I made a pirate costume with a parrot on my shoulder, a patch over my eye, waving a plastic sword, and holding a fake hook with my other hand. Taking the train, not driving, so I could drink, often drawing attention. While traveling is fun, being best dressed for the occasion on a boat party heading out of the harbour was even better. Those were the days, my friend, when I thought the party would never end. But it eventually did, and I outgrew my need to drink and party. Regarding dressing up, I still do that from time to time to capture a bit of the old me. It's too much effort to be dressing up all the time. I'm comfortable being in my PJs when I'm home. Often with zoom calls, I dress my top half and stay in my PJ bottoms. Prior to lockdown, I would've never let myself out in my trackies and trainers. Now, I have no problem, it's all part of being myself.

Having a morning of looking after Janjo's youngest son Jani for about three hours was an absolute pleasure while she took her older boy to school and ran a few errands. Her boys are so affectionate with their hugs and cuddles. I have felt so at home and at peace with them. It's another treasured memory I can use to bring myself into a calm and relaxing state after any stressful situation. All the wonderful memories of loving life and living in the moment.

As I plan the next part of my journey to Wellington, I have the option of an expensive plane ride for an hour and a half, or some ten hours of travelling by bus, sometimes overnight. I hoped that during the long bus ride there would be much writing getting done! This trip I did overnight on a double-decker with bunks, and I had the choice of lying on the mattress or in a net hammock. I chose the latter, being on the bottom bunk was very soothing. Having to go to the toilet was a little difficult as I struggled to get out of the hammock in the dark, searching for my phone to put on the flashlight.

COMING HOME AND THE CHANGE OF LIFE

Arriving back to the town in New Zealand that adopted our refugee family like orphans brought forward a lot of feelings. We came here after leaving a little island that almost doesn't exist anymore, at least not the way it did back then. My birthplace, where I lived for those early years of my life, was never my home.

Now, I was back in Wellington, New Zealand with mixed feelings. In the past, I always felt like it was a sense of being home on my visits back. This time, it had been around three years since I last came back. I wondered if I would fit in immediately after getting off the plane like previously, or would I feel like a fish out of water? This trip felt like a bit of the latter.

Every single one of my regular friends and family whom I had stayed with on previous visits seemed to be busy... *what will I do?*

I felt like there was no need to stress as the universe always looked out for me. My trust in the universe developed to be stronger and more secure over time, and the self-doubt that was once around had disappeared. There was so much more harmony in my thoughts and feelings to help me obtain my more regular peace of mind, and vibrations, that I feel happier than I had been for a very long time. If only I could get my stomach operating better; the bloating, travelling, eating, and the self-discipline of what I fed myself and sticking to healthy eating can be thrown out the window so easily. Not having any regular eating pattern, nor eating a balanced diet, goes totally out the window when travelling. And it seems to be about constantly adjusting as I go along. I have a joke I have referred to in the past, as I lost my period, I gained peace of mind.

It had been four days since I turned sixty-five. Did I feel any different? No, not really. I was the same person but have now aged another year and four days.

I was about to apply for my age pension; filling in forms is the bane of my existence nowadays.

COMING HOME AND THE CHANGE OF LIFE

With filling in most of the questionnaires, the age brackets to tick were typically 56-64—I no longer fit with who I am according to a piece of paper. The next age bracket is typically 65-70 or something like that. There's a ten-year jump in the next box. With each passing year, I am more aware that I'm approaching another big milestone, being 70 years old! I have been very apprehensive about this number getting higher as I'm now starting to feel older. Our bodies can change, along with our minds and point of view on things—so many changes in so many ways. Important things can become less important, and vice versa. As it's often said, life is never meant to be a struggle. I no longer run up the stairs as I did so a few years before. Not sure I can blame this on Covid-19, but it sure hasn't helped.

I do accept reaching the age of retirement. In New Zealand, it's 65, and in Australia, it's 67, and it continues to rise. Filling in questionnaires and forms to request the pension sometimes does my head in. Does getting older mean a higher level of self-awareness and wisdom? Automatically, a higher-level awareness and consciousness, possibly. Or it can be instant stress for some, yet for other people, they seem to age like a fine wine.

Here's one example in particular: my idols, Tina Turner, who is now 78, and Cher, who I just saw perform weeks ago, at 72 with such vigour and vitality when she was in Melbourne. Yes, I am truly realising age is just a number.

Seeing Tina live in concert in 1997, some (well over) 20 years ago in New Zealand was a treat. Tina is 15 years older than me—and her tonality and vibrancy at around 58 at that performance was fantastical and amazing. She wore exquisite clothes that fit her like a glove and contoured her fitness. I saw the beauty within her face and realised nothing was stopping me from being like her, except my own thoughts. Okay, I'll never be as famous as her, but it's only my thoughts that can hold me back from looking and feeling just like her...or a variation of that, anyway. Even today, to me, her dynamic is an inspiration of growing old being only a state of mind.

Aging can be as much an advantage as a disadvantage... it is what it is, a direct result of what we think in our minds. Taking total responsibility to be who I really want to be is all up to me. Once I'm in these higher vibrations, the energy in alliance, with the right actions to be able to attract. It's called the law of attraction when manifestation can take place. If I want my life to be *magical*, then I'm the only person who can do it. If I want help and support it to move, all I must do is ask the universe and stop being wishy-washy in not knowing what I truly want. Find the clarity, in order to be the person, I'm truly destined to be, and create my own reality by trusting the process of the universe!

I want to create my own version of *Eat, Pray, Love* via my own process and journey. Yes, staying in one place might eventually happen; travelling can accelerate the rate of this progress, like the self-realisation of the actress Julia Roberts in the movie of the same name. Just like Julia's character in the film, if I was at home in my usual routine, I couldn't have experienced the interactions with people and situations, the same thoughts and feelings as fast. It would've been different, that's for sure. But it really comes from self-accepting and letting go of the pain often felt as rejection. The more I accepted myself, the less I felt the rejection of others.

Constant movement is my path. If I access my internal GPS, I can get closer, and sometimes it might seem like I am going around in a circle, but in being in the flow, there are better results than staying still and staying stuck. Being fearful of not knowing how to shift can be problematic. There's unity in allowing our heart to be guided and be in alignment with our thoughts, and trusting them, which can be a real battle that exists within the mind.

Stop rushing ahead and trying to get there quicker without doing the planning and research. It's a fine line between one and the other, as I find that if I don't do things under pressure sometimes, it never gets done. But sometimes things need more thoughtful and careful planning. My way is probably a bit chaotic at times, but it does seem to work for me and in my favour, as it is not second-guessing and doubting myself and sometimes I realise I just need to let go and trust in the process, as not being able to let go can cause stress.

Rather than beating around the bush and rambling on, it really boils down to self-acceptance and balancing, head and heart in alignment is my metaphor. Raise above your head with your heart to get an aerial perspective of looking down rather than trying to look up to the sun without wearing the right glasses to tone down the blinding brightness of the sun! Therefore, the unity of thoughts and action makes the heart feel happy and content, a different perspective to view life. Chilling out and enjoying each day as it comes is another one of my mottos.

Don't worry, be happy! I often sing these words to myself if I start to feel stressed.

ANOTHER TRIP

I just landed a few days before my birthday in October, with the two-week mark taking me to the beginning of November. It's interesting how this trip came about. Roger, my ex, passed away suddenly back in June. With my birthday looming, my daughter invited me over to spend it together. So, I saw it as a good time to buy a new laptop to start writing.

As I wrote and thought, I felt more and more each day, week, and month. I felt more balanced, so not many things rocked me the same way they had impacted me in the past. More and more, it's about acceptance.

I headed to Wellington to see one of my closest friends and artist buddies, Andrea, who is like a sister from another mother. Our relationship is a sisterhood closeness that extends next door to Suzy, who has also become a good friend. I remember back in the day when I still enjoyed drinking, we had sleepover parties where I learnt a long-time ago, never to drink and drive.

Staying, I saw just how hectic life was for Andrea with family and caring for pets, she adopted a little blackbird with a broken wing, who she has named Negro. Ipo is the name for her cockatoo. I would like to think that my small input and company with cooking supports her when I stay. She's a fantastic cook that doesn't like cooking anymore. I still have a strong passion, as I love to eat, so I need to cook to be happy. On this trip, I was also somewhat surprised regarding how quick I was to offer to babysit Leo, Di's grandson, whom she is raising solo, so she could attend the party at Sea's (their neighbour's) house. It was an 80s-themed horror movie party where everyone dressed up. I felt as if I had reached a level of maturity where I would view the party enjoy my fascination with dress-ups, but I no longer felt the need to be part of it, no more needing to drink in order to have fun. The pun on the word here is a party at Sea's house, by the sea, as directly across the front of the house was the sea.

I've known Andrea for some years as were fellow students when I went to art school. That's a future story. I haven't been around for her 'Day of the Dead' house exhibition in her home, which have become an annual exhibition. It's a date I'm making a mental note to be there for in the coming years. She hired a professional makeup artist and full costume for the occasion, and if I hadn't seen the before and after face, I might not have even recognised her.

I felt the need to make a definite plan and set into motion a cause and effect to be where I am, and the degree of clarity towards my goal of travelling and dividing my time between two countries, Australia and New Zealand, to live my life as one big holiday between the two countries. Then, every 12 to 18 months, an extra holiday in the UK. See more within the diameter of my three chosen countries, Australia, New Zealand, and the UK. The time is divided by spending five months in both New Zealand and Australia, then six weeks or so in the UK with family there. I have more and more accepted that I can make some plans and let the universe take care of the rest.

I was told it was impossible to live between two counties and that going to a third was an impossible dream. Yet, it was flowing into reality for me. As I felt I finally achieved this, along came the pandemic of Covid-19.

Writing while typing is a great step toward getting closer to my goal. I aim to be finished in the next three to four months and have as much self-editing as possible done to be ready and sent off to the editor, with the goal of being published and launched before or by the third week of April 2019. (Sidenote: I did not achieve my goal but chose to leave this sentence in to see just how long the actual reality takes me).

My new rant/chant is putting my stories out there for an editor, even a book-writing mentor. My goal and dream are to be able to talk and share my 'point to the heart' dim sum stories on a stage platform where I will be paid for my storytelling. That would be a dream come true, and sometimes, I have a light bulb moment of this happening as I edit; it might be possible.

There's a saying that when one is ready, the right teacher will just show up, and this did eventuate for me to be at this point now, but not at the time I was writing this.

I feel very contented to be able to have achieved everything I have thus far, and today is about mapping out what I would like to do and accomplish before I leave Wellington on Sunday to return to Melbourne.

With re-establishing my relationship in Wellington and my old hometown again, I'm excited to see the outcome of my time here. Reap the benefits of getting things done in a short space of time.

FEELING THE FEAR

This next story I would like to share is about 'feeling the fear' and doing it anyway.

I remember my first day of high school when I lived in New Zealand in my early teens. We were dressed in our togs (swimsuit) and told to line up, then climb up the steps, and plunge off the diving board. I do not recall being asked if I knew how to swim or anything; I just wanted to fit in and do what everyone else was doing, all the while forgetting I had no idea that I had a fear of heights, and most of all, I didn't know how to swim. That important fact was overlooked somehow in my naivety.

My sense of adventure and excitement stopped me from worrying or thinking of any consequences. I climbed up without looking down; I didn't even watch how the others were doing it before my turn. I was totally unaware it could and would have been so much better if I had watched and worked out a technique, or even different techniques. It seemed relatively easy once you got to the top. As seen on TV, it looks ever so graceful, or so I thought. I vaguely remember standing on the diving board and thinking, *okay, what do I do next?* I was living so much in the moment, maybe my strong determination was led by my naïve sense of excitement with absolutely no concept of repercussions. I leapt forward and did an almighty horrendous belly flop. I can't quite remember with it being so long ago, but it must have hurt when I hit the water because I remember struggling to not sink. I know I swallowed quite a bit of water.

I can also vaguely remember the shocked and sinking feeling. I was flapping my arms, gasping for breath, and swallowing water. Time seemed to have stood still as I bobbed under the water. It seemed like forever, but eventually, I found my way to the edge of the pool, desperately trying to hang on. Then finally, I heard the teacher saying, "Are you okay?" It seemed a bit late, especially since water was already up my nose. I might have mumbled something, but she *did not* help me out, I was strong enough to pull myself up and out of the pool.

The details seemed clear in my mind, yet a little fuzzy at the same time—it was well over 50 years ago, after all. I did recall that sense of adrenaline and empowerment. It was a thrill and invigorating all at the same time. Yet, to this day, I have not tried it again; I have only jumped in from the side of the pool, feet first.

As an adult in my 30s, I finally learnt how to swim in salt water, in a quiet and calm bay in Queen Charlotte Sound in New Zealand. Sea water gave me natural buoyancy, so it was easy treading in salty sea water, as swimming pools use a lot of chlorine and have no buoyancy at all.

I am the only one of my siblings that ever learnt to swim. Also, none of my siblings learnt how to ride a bike, so doing that gave me a sense of empowerment amongst my siblings. This story is such an epiphany, like many others that have surfaced, in the pool of my life.

MY TRIP TO WEST FOOTSCRAY LIBRARY

I've been having trouble with my Norton Antivirus software while using the public Wi-Fi in the library. It's a slight problem that feels like pulling teeth, but I need to overcome it. And because of this, I haven't really typed or written for almost a week.

I need to solve this problem to get back on track with my dim sum stories.

I need to get the email sent to WINZ in New Zealand and contact Centrelink to let them know I'm back in Australia. Realising all this, it seems I might need to be working at the local library again every day. I need to see the computer tutor at Footscray Library, or someone here at my local West Footscray branch to get some more techy advice.

I am going to sing with the West Footscray, or WEFO, choir at the Maidstone Community Centre every second Wednesday. This is the last practice before our performance next Saturday. I have journaled some words for today and need to write, and if needed because of the Wi-Fi issues, I'll go back to pen to paper for a bit until I sort out this hiccup.

The sudden death of a close friend has affected me a bit more than I thought it would. We used to hang out together when I first arrived in Melbourne, and then we lost touch after she married. To hear on social media she passed away suddenly, without knowing why or how, was hard. It reminds me how short life is. I just need to get on with my goals to achieve them and stop my procrastination.

HEART FELT LIKE A MAORI

L ast night was so cold that I slept in all my clothes.

I had a lovely breakfast with my close friend Andrea and then started what should have been a 10-minute walk to the airport, but however so many closed-off areas, it took an extra 10 minutes to find my way through a maze of metal fences. I had a lovely few days in Wellington and was looking forward to heading to Auckland. Flying from Wellington to Auckland is equivalent to flying from Melbourne to Sydney.

Sarah, my old friend, and previous massage client from over 20 years ago, picked me up. From there, we had some lovely food as the food on the plane was limited. I bought a snack for my bus trip to Kerikeri for $37 on the plane. The cost of this flight with a 10 kg carry-on was $84. Travel is expensive but better if one's organised and prepared. It was not worth enduring hours on a bus there, but I did on leaving as it gave me a variety in a scenic way, of seeing the countryside without the stress of driving. I investigated taking a train but that was even more expensive.

I aimed to get a lot more writing done while I stayed with Hopi and Don, old family friends from the early 1970s whom I met via Roger.

I aimed to return on Monday 21st as I offered to give a cooking lesson in Makara Wellington on Tuesday for the two teenage granddaughters where I have house sat. I can sort the last of my things while there. I only have five boxes left of everything I had in my last house. Then Wednesday, I move to another place where it's closer for me to bus into the central business district to see Nigella Lawson at the Michael Fowler Centre. It was interesting, she was sitting in an armchair in the centre of the stage, talking and answering questions. It was so different from seeing her on her cooking shows on TV. Meeting her and getting her autograph on her latest cookbook was wonderful. But on TV, she seems far more vivacious, even a little solemn, in a white dress, bare of any jewellery on a lone armchair, front centre stage.

It was so easy picking up where I left off with dear old friends from the early 1970s, something I can often do with special people in my life. Hopi looked fantastic, the skinniest she has ever looked, and had just turned 70 years young. As Hopi has battled with weight most of her life, she introduced me to the Keto way of eating. No carbs, loads of proteins. I found it difficult after a few weeks of losing only 6 kg, so I abandoned this diet. I'm an addict when it comes to carbs to fill me. My body doesn't seem to like too much protein after years of trying different diets to keep my weight in check.

Wednesday 16th, we went into town, and I found the op shops while Don and Hopi went to the doctor. I always love exploring op shops wherever I go. I have finally learnt to shop with my eyes only unless I really need it. I now seem to have less clutter than I used to living in a traditional house with so many bedrooms to myself to fill. I now have the motto, less suits me better than more.

All my friends and I have always celebrated when coming together; we cook together, a feast of some form. The first night was a big stir fry of vegetables, butter, and parsley giant prawns, very decadent. On Thursday, I went to Waitangi with Don and Hopi, where I felt transported back in time. They took me on the whole tourist experience. Māori culture is an integral part of life in Aotearoa, New Zealand. For millennia, Māori have been the Tangata Whenua, the Indigenous people of Aotearoa, which means 'people of the land.' Waitangi is the place where the treaty of Waitangi was signed, the crown the exclusive right to buy the Māori land. I have loved history and that of the indigenous culture since my first exposure to it in primary school upon my arrival in New Zealand.

Waitangi is where history was made, unknown to the Māori nation, the land ownership was taken for the price of a few riffles and blankets. They had no idea they had passed over ownership at that time. Sad history here, learning how badly Maori children were treated even up until the early 1960s

There was an entry fee and a gala performance, which is right up my alley as I love song and dance. There was a performance of traditional singing and dancing. The richness of the voices, the poi swinging, and watching traditional Haka—vigorous and emotional movements of stamping and stomping the feet—was thrilling. The Haka was their way of scaring off the enemy, showing their strength and power now used to mark a celebration. A rhythmic chant and dance that once only men were allowed to perform and women were forbidden. People have now been allowed to see women and men performing together on the site where the original treaty was signed. I enjoyed immersing myself in the Māori culture on this trip, taking many photos and videos with my smartphone.

On Friday, I took more photos of this fantastic escape, a holiday of historical delights that I have never seen before. I went to the meeting house, traditionally called a Marae, located in a sacred area, each panel on the inside is carved and tells a story. On entry, it's customary to take your shoes off.

One of my Māori spiritual teachers in the early 1990s took us, her students, to our first Marae visit. The visit instantly resonated with me. We all slept together on the floor of the meeting house; a tradition done even when it was often hard to get any sleep with the amount of snoring going on. My best memory was participating in a dawn ceremony.

We dressed in our best clothes, walked in a single line with torches and stood in the dark, awaiting the dawn.

Although I might not understand more than a few words of the Māori language, my soul still felt completely at home being there—that sense of feeling totally at peace. It was a genuinely unforgettable and remarkable, soulful experience to treasure.

Calling in of the special day of remembrance, I had on my moving back to my hometown. I went on a trip with one of my two, Māori spiritual teachers to her home Marae when our group was having a late-night meditation session in the European-style church (we kept our shoes on) that was there on another part of the Marae. On coming out at around midnight, I saw the vision of a statue of Pania. At the time I said to myself that I wanted to see the statue in daylight tomorrow, but it wasn't there the next day, and a few other members of our group had this same vision. Pania of the Reef, a statue of this name, stands on the foreshore of Napier's Marine Parade. I saw this vision years before I travelled to Napier on a visit some 12 years ago, yet this memory is stored in my heart's photo album.

WOMAN WARRIOR

Today was an exciting day.

When I entered the Footcray library to do some typing, a woman came up to me and asked if I was a Māori as I was wearing a tiki (a charm worn around the neck for protection, like the Greek evil eye). It was an honour, and my spiritual mana both shone and reflected. Hearing what she said made my day…my week…my life.

I have had this saying for a while now, "I am Chinese born, but my spirit is that of a Māori."

During my reading and research, I have found that to change ourselves, we need to begin by being aligned with our minds' thoughts. I have thought about that for a long time now. I like to live with the saying: I want to go with the flow. I want to create the right vibrations and become the person I think I am, the person I am destined to be. I guess I have been re-designing who I am, to reinvent myself, and it's finally starting to happen. I am attracting things in my life I have had in my mind for a long time. I have lived life and learnt to be patient, but I also know I must put it out there and ask the universe.

Every day I have this tuning-in to be in touch with my inner being, to be the very best I am in my interactions with people to contribute to the harmony of the day ahead. In getting older, I feel less and less self-doubt; I feel so much more comfortable in my skin. I listen to my inner voice and pace myself in my activities, so I don't burn out, as I have been known to do this.

It's interesting how I have become more introspective and no longer find it necessary to be rushing around trying to do everything. I weigh up how many hours I spend out of the house on social activities, and then how many hours I want to spend time with moi (myself). I'm eager to get home and be with myself when I have been out for so long. I feel as if I have finally found the love for myself, the love I have yearned for so long. I have been alone for a long time, and I feel some of it was fear of being hurt and losing trust outwardly. I have spent this period of one-ness (not aloneness) developing a much deeper relationship with myself. So, in a way, I have become my own lover. It's a gift that I have begun to give to myself—treating myself with more love and respect.

I plan my day out and aware that things change, and I adjust my schedule to get the most out of each day, all the while being mindful to listen to my inner child, within reason. Such as, having ice cream for breakfast once in a blue moon is a way I can nurture my inner child, but the adult in me reasons that my digestive system cannot handle the shock too often. I reckon when I was younger, I had a cast iron gut and could eat anything and everything I wanted without ever having any side effects, this is no longer the case as I have gotten older.

I also wanted to see a movie today but realised I needed to catch up with more important things—*better done today rather than tomorrow, like getting a haircut*. My hair has been getting hard to tame, blowing wildly out of place in the wind. I walked into my hairdresser, and she was free, so my intuition to do it today rather than tomorrow was spot on. However, sometimes when there are too many people waiting, I walk away and try again on another day.

A good hairdresser is hard enough to find, but a cheap one as well, now that's a treasure. My Vietnamese hairdresser only charged me $12. Back in New Zealand, before moving countries, even with a friend who gave me 'mates rates' it was at least $40 whereas a basic haircut in Melbourne was at least around $70 or more, and I was told this was the average rate in Melbourne. I chatted with other people who were waiting, they travelled from

Carlton. I have stayed with this hairdresser for so many years to find she had disappeared after lockdown.

My local shopping is done in Footscray, still my favourite place when I need anything, as it's only about, a 20-30 minute walk from home. Not like when I lived in the New Zealand countryside, taking almost an hour to get into town. I rarely bothered with haircuts, then grew my hair long instead, like in true hippie tradition.

My joy in singing is the reason for being in Melbourne.

Every week I headed into the city of Melbourne for our choir rehearsals. I like to meet up with my friends and somehow ended up forming a close friendship with a blind member. I wanted to pick up my blind friend off the train as the roadworks outside the station were crazy at the time. Despite having a seeing-eye dog, entering the station that was temporarily in renovation could be chaotic. Brandon is an amazingly independent lad in his early 20s and has a great singing voice. He also plays blind soccer. Now I know you might be thinking, *how is that possible*? I find it amazing, and he plays blind tennis as well. I am so in awe as it's a big handicap not being able to see, achieving success that even with eyes have difficulties with.

When I last spoke to him, he told me he was going to America to represent Australia in the Blind Olympics.

I felt much better meeting up with him at the station and walking to St Michael's for choir rehearsal, then taking him back afterwards due to the obstacles. He's so independent and a determined achiever. He has since left the choir to focus on his studies and to play blind soccer. When I last spoke with him, when I asked his permission to use his name, he was heading overseas to represent Australia playing blind soccer—I have trouble kicking a ball with sight. Such an amazing young man I had the honour of singing and spending time with. We have a phone catchup every now and then. He was 23 then. It's great to have a friendship with someone even younger than my children. In fact, he's only a few years older than my grandson.

The mother in me is very proud of the child within. An exciting realisation to come to terms with regarding *acceptance*. I can feel like a child again, and the mother comes forth to care for and nourish the inner child that was hurt—to be my own mother to care for the hurt child within. So, like a child that wants to do everything, but sometimes fails to get much done at all. I love going to see movies on a big screen, beats watching on a TV at home any day.

I had the fantasy of quickly taking the groceries I bought home and still having time to head out to see a movie as it was the cheap day and the only venue showing *Bohemian Rhapsody*. I had to let go, and the writing flowed as I began composing in my mind that I wanted to put pen to paper. To get home quickly and utilise my creative juices. I decided it was best to go back home and stay at home conserve some energy for the next day. Sometimes, the child in me wants to do so many things, and because of that, I often forget my limits. In the aging process, I have become less fit, so when I do overdo things, I pay the price with aches and pains and lower energy, I cannot accomplish anything if I burn out, a lesson I learnt the hard way.

I see this as learning to balance the child in me and balancing the adult to fine-tune that to reach a happy balance.

I often used to think I wanted to do everything; maybe I could've been like Superwoman some 25 to 30-odd years ago. Expecting that growing old is inevitable. I cannot avoid it but to be able to do it with the utmost grace. Part of my growing up and finding maturity was realising my own abilities and strengths, and the need to adjust accordingly and not burn out by overdoing things. The saying goes, it takes wise, small actions to achieve big results. Too much grand action often can get small results. So, acting smartly and wisely, with next to no effect, is like becoming a magician in the art of living! This is the description of me in being a warrior, my term for being brave in Speaking up. Understanding my own limits more.

EATING MY WAY AROUND THE WORLD IN ONE DAY

This morning, I woke up and felt like Italian for breakfast, so I made vongole pasta, which is Italian for *clam pasta*. I always make my own sauce from scratch but wanted to try a new Latina jar sauce, as I didn't have the time or energy to spend a long time preparing. I very rarely use pre-made sauces but picked a great one; it even tasted homemade, which was a real surprise. Gluten-free pasta also seems to cook faster than the wheat range. For the frozen clams, I cooked with a little pasta sauce, spring onions, and some olive oil, so I had to reduce the liquid to thicken the sauce.

I did some yoga stretches before lunch at 2 pm to justify such a big-big breakfast. Spanakopita, a cottage cheese-like pie and Bourkouri, which is a burghul wheat pilaf, is a Sicilian dish. Then train and tram to meet my friends at a Turkish restaurant where we had a six-course banquet, celebrating a birthday. It was middle eastern food, not too spicy at all which was a relief because as I have gotten older, I can't handle spices like I used to when I was younger.

In my late teens and early 20s, I ate chillies for breakfast. When my kids were little, they didn't like spices, now it's the reverse: I can't handle too hot and spicy foods, but they love everything with a hot hit that bangs on the tongue and leaves that lingering heat. Even my seven-year-old grandson loves extra hot spicy foods. I had Italian today to feel closer to my Italian family.

I love shared eating with others, I find it gives so much more variety. Thus, I ate myself part way around the world in one day. Sometimes, I don't eat many Chinese foods, and other times, I might. I often say my taste buds are multicultural.

THE VIRTUAL WORLD

I'm experiencing a new experience today.

I'm in a virtual classroom, in the comfort of my living room.

Listening to instructions is so easy to apprehend, but at times, mind-boggling. It's a virtual room full of strangers who are my potential friends. Two years ago, if someone told me I would be sitting here in this class, I would have never believed it to be possible. Life is about trying new things. As the saying goes, "You cannot do the same thing over and over again and expect different results."

It seems like my own million-dollar question that I will have to find my answers to as well. What is the question I have up front? I didn't know what to expect, and there was a sense of wonderment, the feeling of mystery, to see how the day unfolds. Hearing other people's points of view, seeing their faces, knowing them through their words, and figures of speech. It has shown me possibilities to learn from each person, not just copy them but to take highlights of what they share to adapt to where I am currently standing. I want to be open to change, to explore, and live new things from a different point of view. I want to go back to being that inquisitive child, asking endless questions to the point of being obsessive! But is there a point in being a bit more mysterious? Does that capture more readers, or is it their hearts I want to be able to open?

Looking outside my window, everything seems still and a little quiet now, when some half-hour ago there was a continuous barking and agitated dog, somewhere very close, maybe the next street. Right now, I can hear the soft singing of the birds outside, whereas before, they were so much noisier, all trying to voice themselves at once. The dog and the birds were noisy chatterboxes for a while, then almost dropped to a quiet, silence.

The sound, or lack of sound, has a guidance about it that seems like we might still be in lockdown. The little burst of bird songs, and the distant sound of cars, interrupted by a train's engine rushing with the very occasional toot, toot.

A truly unforgettable day, totally alien and out of my norm to start learning online, a new experience, that will be happening frequently over the next two years and more.

FUK LUK SAU

This is my story of the three wise men, who were also known as the three stars that took on human form, and my interest in coming across them to learn more. My parents owned their first set, and when they upgraded to a nicer set, I was given the original. I remembered them proudly, standing guard when I visited them when they were taken out of an old camphor chest. They were brought over to New Zealand, carefully wrapped with clothing and blankets to keep them safe, in cargo when we sailed from Hong Kong, a long sea journey.

There seems to be a similarity with some Greek mythology, as the stories that come from my ancestral country.

Fuk Luk Sau are figurines that stand guard to protect the home. So many Asian businesses have them in their shop as a shrine. For a fun and interesting fact, they stand around 12 inches high. I grew up with them on the family mantle watching over us.

It was part of the inheritance, or rather what I chose, on my mother's passing. All I knew were their names and what they represented: abundance, long life, and wealth.

My parents had two sets: the first set was made of plastic and the second they purchased in later years was made from porcelain. It was the original set that was passed on to me. I later inherited them both. I left them both in storage with the last few items I have still back in New Zealand. As a child, I barely took any notice, I only really started to find them interesting after my mother passed away.

These three wise men are my link with my parents and my ancestry. I researched the history to find they were advisors to the Emperor during the Ming Dynasty—from 1368-1644—which was quite a lengthy reign. Ming is my mother and daughter's name. That gave me even more enthusiasm to explore further.

I am deepening my understanding of my heritage, and I am ashamed to say I seem to have so little knowledge of my own culture. It was my interest in history that brought on my fascination to unfold and find out more.

From my reading, these guys were like Merlin, the adviser to King Arthur. With world history, there are links throughout the time that often has a connection to history. In conclusion, there didn't seem to be as much information, yet there's a fascination of being able to connect that every country seems to have folklore that has a similar storyline.

Choir on tour in Uluru

Dinner Party

Pahautane People 1975

First cooking school

Fuk Luk Sau

Me aged 42

Me and Ipo

Me at 23 years old

Me In Egypt

Me In Greece

Me In Jordan

My Initiation to Budhism

Me with snake

Grilled Octopus

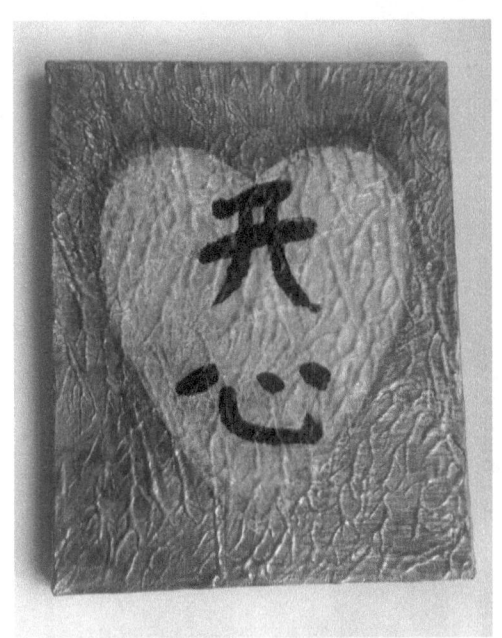

Open heart

Old Business Card

Me as a Pirate

Choir

Me in the Middle East

Lentil as Anything

ODE TO LOVE

This is the story of my first love, and where following my heart led; it reminds me of the old Carol King song, *Where You Lead, I'll Follow.*

In Wellington, New Zealand, on the North Island, I met him just as he was buying into some land on the west coast of the South Island.

I went to stay a week with him to say goodbye. It was just a visit to him on the land before I took off overseas on my travels. But it ended with me blindly following my heart, never leaving until almost 18 years later. This is about my experience of my very first love. The only man I have ever loved and trusted, and somehow ended up losing myself in the process. There were some good points and some massive lessons and learnings.

Some months after we got together, maybe a year, he told me that he chose me as I seemed like an innocent swan. On reflection, this was a bit of a shock, thinking that he thought I would be submissive.

I didn't know how to react, whether to see it as a compliment or an insult. And in his own words: "I was shocked when I asked you on the first night we were together if you had a condom." If I was wiser, I would have seen this as a sign; he didn't have protection, but he wanted sex. This was the very first sign of his disrespect. If I was smarter and wiser, I would have seen that. That's why I say I was blinded by love.

Yes, I felt the same attraction, but not to take responsibility for unprotected sex. He said I was an innocent flower. I was young at the time, barely 20 years old when we met.

I saw him behaving like a monkey, climbing on a barred window cell. He was stoned and *out of it* on weed—and I remember thinking how silly this guy looked, acting like an ape. But I was also fascinated and rebellious. It was the beginning of falling in love.

I was brought up in the Chinese Anglican Church. And he was a roadie of a popular band, with long blondish hair well past his shoulders and the loveliest blue eyes that made my heart melt. It was easy to mistake him from the back as a woman, except for his broad surfing shoulders. It took me a while to tell the difference between him and his three friends, kind of like the saying that all Asians look the same; well, so do men with long hair and beards! My naïve-ness indeed.

Hippie, this was a new word. I just started hearing about the famous music festival, *Woodstock*. He told me he took his mother to the documentary movie of the same name and made hash brownies. In a new era, I came across a group of mainly guys as my sister, who was three years younger than I. She was already dating the drummer of this band. I was sure she was sleeping with him, too, but we weren't close enough for her to share intimate details about her losing her virginity.

One of the local hangouts was a little music shop called Grass Tracks. With some out-of-this-world beats. I fell head over heels; it was new and fascinating, and it was my first experience of *love*. It was different from my previous crushes and admirations: guys from school, and a Chinese boy my brother's age that played in a band and dressed like The Beatles in the Sargent Peppers period. It was just an infatuation. At 18, I lost my virginity as a challenge I wanted to experience rather than a heartfelt encounter. I was seduced by an illusion that was like a grade I had to accomplish.

When Roger and I met, I was on the verge of going travelling to follow my Indian guru who was about to open an Ashram in Hong Kong, my birth country. I had to surrender my passport for my traditional old-school mother to allow me to leave home instead of going overseas. She didn't trust me I moved into the Ashram, the centre and house of devotees, where some of the occupants were somewhat permissive. Roger came to stay with me there for a few days before he moved to his land on the South Island that he and his sister bought with her then-husband. This piece of land was maybe 3000 acres they purchased for $36,000 with financial help from their parents.

That was an exciting time of *free love*, also called 'partner swapping'. Roger and I made it very clear we would only stay exclusive to each other.

Many couples ended up splitting up as they fell in love with someone else who was not the other parent of their children. It got messy for some of the kids in the neighbourhood.

Roger then told me to go travelling, and he would wait for me to return. I was pretty sure it had the opposite effect because if he told me he didn't want me to go, I would have. As I said, he was the love of my life, and we wanted to cement our love by having a baby right away. I knew the moment and the split second I conceived; it was on the drive home from the city, back to the country on train tracks, somewhere around Arthur's Pass, after a live concert of the Mahavishnu Orchestra on route home from Christchurch, back to the West Coast.

Roger, in comparison to me, had a totally different life experience. At the age of 18, he hitchhiked all over America barefoot, carrying only a sleeping bag and the book of the prophet. He met an American woman who was some seven years older whom he lived with and married on the insistence of her extremely strict Catholic parents, who refused to even meet him unless they were married. Anyway, he brought her to New Zealand after some time, but their relationship fell apart. When that happened, she moved back to the USA without getting divorced.

I was too young and naive to even realise I was in love with a *married* man. I can remember when we told his parents once it was confirmed I was pregnant. The first thing they said—asked—was if we were going to get married. Roger said yes, but he had to get a divorce first. This took four years before he chickened out because he said he felt forced. However, in the meantime, we'd already had a second child.

Upon reflection, it seems funny that he got married twice; our relationship was between the two legal marriages, and it, I that bore him two children. His only children were with me, his defacto.

As a half measure, for the kids going to school and his elected position in local government, we decided as a compromise I would have my name changed by his good friend and former lawyer, who gave up law to be a mechanic. We thought for his political reputation, it would be best for me to share the same last name with him and the children. For some 17-odd years, I went under the name Helene Brookes. That name seems so alien to me now a quarter of a century later before I de-polled it back to my birth name.

WALKING ON BROKEN GLASS

I have often woken up drunk from my sleep—not from drinking alcohol—to find broken glass on my kitchen floor.

I thought how lucky I was to be in a space of such relaxation, that I have the freedom to be me. In a place I don't need to explain myself to anyone, nor worry what others might think and how I might be judged, as I no longer give a dam.

What I mean by walking on broken glass is, and I share two cases with you…

This first one was when I realised I never needed to *people-please* again, and how liberating it is.

It's taken me years to find this freedom in my actions rather than walking on broken glass. I recently knocked over a glass full of runny sauce, and I could not deal with the clean-up for almost two days. This is how I came to this awareness of how I deal with certain relationships in my life, dealing with delicate situations.

In my personal case, I got home hungry quite late one night. And in my tiredness, I knew it would be impossible to fall asleep when I was hungry. It was almost midnight when it happened, and I thought there was no way I could deal with it at the time. In the morning, I woke with only just enough time to get myself off for a busy day, and I knew it was a delicate situation I needed time and patience to be able to deal with it, so, I avoided and tip-toed around the broken glass for days. I compared this to life's situations and our avoidance of dealing with certain situations. How many times in the past would I probably have sworn and been angry with myself for being so clumsy? In this case, my metaphor, and in some cultures, it's good luck, and in others bad luck.

Thus, pointless and meaningless to be superstitious.

Knocking on wood, throwing salt over your shoulders, walking under a ladder, a broken mirror, and stepping on a crack…old wife's tales. There's a horseshoe and crossing your fingers for good luck.

I'm also referring to not being able to speak about how bad living in a bad situation can be. It could be like walking on broken glass.

So interesting how we can shelve situations in our life with this metaphor. I also compared it to being under the same roof with my daughter and her partner of seventeen years, who have separated but had to try and communicate without really communicating.

So interesting spending time with family and looking back to evaluate and reflect. More and more, I can see the time and energy we waste on trying too hard to make the situation work with my family.

How to learn to speak in a way that is clearly understood and not misunderstood.

There were times in my past when I constantly wanted to do the right thing for others but left myself out in the cold. Now, I speak out and often can get pushback due to being too outspoken in my opinion.

When, all I ever wanted was to have a voice and to be heard.

BOURKE STREET MALL DISASTER AVOIDED

I intended to be in Bourke Street Mall one day in 2017, but something in my stomach told me not to go. Something in my gut stopped me from getting off the bus, instead saying, "Go home." My feet and legs felt like lead for some reason as well.

Usually, I attended a Chi Gong class in the city every Friday morning and would afterwards have some social time over food and coffee. Often, I would also head to the Bourke Street Royal Arcade to visit Magog and Gog, the animated statues guarding the entry of the arcade since 1870. The Gaunt, a specially designed clock that triggers the arms of father time, made by a Melbourne clockmaker at the time, had also been there since 1870.

I loved spending time at this mall. There is a crystal and spell shop there I used to visit and put a coin in to spin the wheel of fortune, but since the tragedy and due to our lengthy extended lockdown, I realised it had been three years since I was last there.

Recently, I found the news story from the day I intended to go to the mall. It's important to be able to write down the details. I needed to recall my memories of that momentous day. That day changed many people's lives, and the fact that it could have been me in the wrong place at the wrong time was frightening.

The whole event itself was only eight minutes! The driver of a stolen car outside Flinders' Street Station was reported on the news to be doing burnouts earlier that morning. There was footage of two brave young men with a baseball bat trying to smash the windscreen to stop the driver when he was driving like a madman outside Flinders Street Station.

Earlier that morning, people saw the driver's strange behaviour in the suburbs. Reportedly, he attacked his brother much earlier that morning before taking off in the stolen car. There was a question after a call to the police; instead of direct action, they chose to monitor him from the air in an outer Melbourne suburb. There was a helicopter following him from above, following him as he drove into the CBD. He was under the illusion that the world was about to end. His crazy actions were his claims to warn people.

BOURKE STREET MALL DISASTER AVOIDED

It was the school holidays, and the city was bustling with activity. The news footage showed the afterwards shots, and amazingly enough, a reporter was close by doing an interview.

There was an overturned pram and a young nanny in a panic to find the children in her care.

There was a 60-minute television program that interviewed witnesses. A paramedic saw a young girl tossed in the air as high as the shop awning before falling back down like a rag doll. I'm so glad I wasn't there as witnessing that scene would have been permanently burnt into my brain. It's a sight I'm so relieved to not have seen with my own eyes. One was the former police commissioner, who witnessed the whole eight minutes of this ordeal. Apparently, there were 100 special forces surrounding the area as they thought it was a terrorist attack, believing the city was under siege. I saw this news footage.

It also happened that a reporter, who was interviewing a politician on the rooftop of one of the shops, was able to capture so many details of what happened on camera.

Another interview was with a woman who had lost her husband. Seeing her being interviewed with such a brave face, I wonder how she could have found the strength. This woman talked about having met her husband earlier that day to have lunch together, and afterwards, she returned to work. Many co-workers were watching the news on television, which set the alarm bell for her to call her husband. Unfortunately, she got no reply from him, which further raised her alarm bell. Her husband's body was too mangled, so the only way she could ID him was from his wedding ring. That day, she became a widow, and her young daughter lost a father.

The day's horrific events changed the lives of so many people as a national disaster. My mind still boggles in realising I could have been there, and my life could have ended. It still shocks me to this day. I'm in awe of how I felt I was warned not to go there on that day. That day changed my perspective on going there for the fun of it. It took me a year to revisit the mall. It's no longer on my list of festive activities in the city. I still go into the city often, walk past and sometimes even forget what happened. I thank the lucky stars that I'm here to tell my story, not end up as a statistic.

The sad fact is that this could have been prevented with the perpetrator serving time. He was in custody previously but was released before he completed his whole sentence as authorities didn't think he was a danger or a threat. It was stated by the media that if he had been monitored better, this terrible incident may not have occurred. The events of Bourke Street are something that continues to shock me!

LIBRARY LOVERS' DAY

Library Lovers' Day: what a great way to celebrate a day that, in the past, has been deemed a day of romance; Valentine's Day, the 14th of February, at Footscray library.

Well, it's only a mere perception of how and where we find love. For us singletons, how awesome is it that we can find love in the library? And the love for me is my desire to write about the experiences from this workshop to catapult me into being a writer.

Coming from a place and a background of a culture where there has been no priority made to encourage reading and hanging out in libraries, I feel as though I found a place to explore the world.

The library has opened its doors to my adventurous appetite to read and research my passions in all there forms, like travelling and extending my understanding of the world beyond what I had grown up with. Born in an Asian country, English was my second language and it has taken me years to build my love affair and thirst to expand my horizons. Travelling to different suburbs to find a library to spend time in is my ideal holiday from everyday life. It's so fascinating how once we used a dictionary and a book, and now have a keyword and the use of the internet. I can research everything and anything that takes my fancy. I am too lazy to find where my old Oxford Dictionary is when it's easy just to pick up my phone and use Google. Google is another thing that's quickly becoming another best friend of mine.

During the summer, I love sitting in a library; it has air conditioning and feels luxurious compared to my stuffy brick apartment, without air-conditioning.

I find time at any library brings me not only joy and happiness but free entertainment too. I travel to many countries via Wi-Fi. My library card is like a passport, taking me places in my head where I can lose myself. The wealth of knowledge at my fingertips is a powerful thing.

I have spent a fortune paying for courses, and at the library, I can get so much information and help from the friendly staff for free, all with a smile. I have found my love for words.

The human relationship has its challenges. I always find it relaxing to spend quality quiet time; it fills my life with joy. I would say my trips to the library are the best.

LIGHTING OF CANDLES

My driving adventures around the Greek islands were a lot of fun. It was where I gathered the courage to rent a car and drive solo. In *most* parts of Europe, they drive on the other side of the road, and the steering is on the other side too. Australia and New Zealand are some of the few places that drive on the left-hand side, while Greece drives on the right.

Hiring a car on my own was a big act of courage; nothing beats fear more than just feeling the fear and doing it!

The car was a Suzuki Panda, and I often slept in it with locked doors, using my clothes as a pillow and a beach towel as a blanket. I wasn't brave enough to sleep on the soft sandy beaches as there were often mosquitoes and sandflies. Staying some nights in the car happened by accident at first, as I got tired quickly before I reached the next town. I felt safe sleeping in my car, and it also meant

I was saving money. At the time, it seemed courageously adventurous. A brave and spontaneous act I've realised that if I thought it over back then in full, I might have chickened out. Reflecting on it now, I followed my heart, and somehow, it seemed safe, and I was looked after by the universe as I totally trusted it.

I followed my nose and talked to the shopkeepers at the local supermarkets about where I should go next while I was picking up water for my trip. I never bought more than a litre at a time as it would end up too warm to drink. At times, the refrigerated water I bought in the supermarkets was a big bonus on a hot day, it would often stay cooler that little bit longer. Although hot, the heat in Greece was so much kinder, that often, I didn't even use any sunblock at all. There was more of an ozone layer, meaning I got really brown and tanned, but never sunburnt. Often back home in New Zealand or Australia, I can get sunburnt in as little time as 15 minutes.

While at the supermarket, I heard there was a Chinese restaurant I should check out. It was exciting news from a shopkeeper who spoke lego English, and with my lego Greek, we communicated well. Lego is the Greek word for a little.

Looking back on how impulsive I was with little research or planning of where I was going, I followed my nose and went with the flow. Nobody knew where I was with my lust for adventure—even the possible danger of travelling alone. If I came to any demise, I wonder now if I could have been identified. Nobody was expecting me, I had no schedule. My thinking, or lack of, seemed not to be blinded by any fear whatsoever. I was crazy now on more reflection, but I was a little wiser afterwards. And with further thinking, I believe that sometimes overthinking things blocks them from ever happening.

Sighting a church up some steps drew me to stop, light a candle, and give a few coins in a donation for safe travelling, which was something I did most days on the road.

I remember when I got to the church, there seemed to be a *closed* sign, but the door was open when I first spotted it. I will speak further about this later in this story.

Then, I went to the Chinese restaurant.

The place was set up quite differently than the local taverna-style open café. Indoors, I spoke with my limited Greek and found out this family migrated from Cambodia. I asked if they spoke any Cantonese, and it turned out the father did, a man in his 60s. He was born in Canton, travelled and met his wife while on an adventure to seek a new way of life in another land, and ended up moving to Greece. His life seemed fascinating. He hadn't spoken his native tongue for over 40 years and was so joyful we could converse. They were about to sit down for lunch as they were usually only open in the evenings, and they insisted I stay and join them.

I don't remember much about the food itself, but it had some familiar flavours. The change from Greek street food was welcoming, just like this family who didn't know me from a bar of soap. Later I realised it was the same but different from the local ingredients. After a satisfying and tasty meal, I offered to pay but they refused to take any money from me and said how refreshing it was to meet me, it was likewise for me. The Chinese have a saying that giving and receiving is a cycle that they refuse any payment of money but accept a gift. Travelling via Sydney, I went to Paddington Market, like the Queen Victoria Market in Melbourne.

At the time of this trip, my home was still in New Zealand, where I started my journey by visiting some friends in Sydney. I love markets and like to have a wide choice of different sunglasses. Little did I know that back then, fashion choices of sunglasses would become so handy on these occasions.

The same happened when I had a flat tyre only to find the spare was already flat.

I was driving down a remote narrow road. Some areas seemed like a single lane only with an occasional spot for another car passing.

LIGHTING OF CANDLES

I noticed the door was open when I passed a church that was up many steep steps but by the time I parked the Panda and walked up the steps, the door was closed and locked. Walking down, I saw a small fountain at the bottom of the steps. It was hot, and I bent down to scoop up some blessed water to splash onto my face.

I then noticed my back tyre was flat, and when I checked the spare in the boot, it was also flat. Asking at local shops, I found a garage down the road. The mechanic didn't speak any English, but with my *lego, lego* (little, little) Greek, he knew what I needed. It seemed like an unspoken understanding.

I had a brief stopover in Vietnam before Greece, where I picked up a couple of cartons of cigarettes as they were *going for a song*. There is a saying that when something is *cheap* it goes for a *song*, and being a singer, I love using this term. So, when he wouldn't take any money, I gave him a few packs, and he seemed very happy, his beaming smile told me of his happiness. Although cigarettes were cheap in Greece, especially back then, the fact that what I had was foreign made them more interesting. The people I met gave me the nickname 'The Little Chinese Greek.'

What was amazing was that with the drive all downhill, I could have met with a nasty accident if I had not seen the car's flat tyre. So, it was worth lighting the candles for my safe travels and protection every day.

LIVING OFF THE SMELL OF AN OILY RAG

I like to say I know where I can shop for a fraction of the price, know what days have cheap products, and the best time to go to the fresh food markets.

When I moved into a new area in Melbourne, I loved being adventurous and exploring the different fresh produce, the days, and the time of the day to get the best bargains. Now there's only Footscray Market. This fresh local market closes on Sundays and Mondays, so late Saturday from 3:30 pm until 4:30 pm when they close was often when I found huge if not massive reductions. And often, it can be fun just listening to the store holder sing their shouting/selling their wares.

My favourite was Little Saigon Market. It was like being in Saigon, one of my visitors from New Zealand said.

It burnt down during one of my trips overseas, and the smell of the rotten food continued for months afterwards.

If you have ever been to an auction, the markets can resemble that atmosphere. And for me, personally, it's not every day I can have the headspace to listen to such noisy screaming. It's often yelled out in pidgin English, like another language. This is often used for not being able to speak with the right tonality and takes a little adapting for the normal ear. Footscray Market is smaller and nowhere near as exciting as Little Saigon. These days, Footscray is very predominantly Vietnamese and Filipino, while once upon a time it was a predominately Italian area.

It can be a mixture of Asian languages, often more men than women promoting what they need to get rid of in a hurry as their store is closed for two days and often more if it aligns with the public holidays. For me, an hour until closing time is the best time to pick up the fresh stuff—meat, vegetables, and fish, the last one having a shorter shelf life. I have, in the past, been caught out buying more than I can use, which is not great because fish *has* such a small shelf/fridge life. I found that cooking and freezing is the best way to avoid wastage.

Often the different stores try to outdo the neighbouring vendors by dropping their prices just that little bit more. I like exploring, hunting and finding such attractive and fun stuff, from food to nice knick-knacks.

Some of my fondest memories were going to the markets after a gym class. That's when the big Saigon Market was still running and open seven days a week. Yes, those were the days I could get bags of fruit and loads of vegetables for $1 or $2 each per pack. It's still, after six years, currently a fenced-off eyesore. Those were the days when I could literally, "Live on a smell of an oily rag."

I remember going when I was hungry especially. Still, my favourite is the Saigon.

Most stores have a plate of fruit sliced or peeled for buyers to have a little taste. I can often have a complimentary fruit salad breakfast by roaming from stall to stall. Snacking on a piece of fruit here and another bit there. It was a whole block.

The current Footscray Market is less than a quarter in size and even less than a quarter amount of adventure and excitement as the old Saigon Market at Footscray.

I miss this great market. During my first year living in Melbourne, I brought a friend who travelled to Saigon. She told me, it felt like going back to relive her holiday. So, one of my bucket list goals is to experience this for myself as I love going on food adventures, especially the street food markets to buy and eat in. Saigon is still on my bucket list.

As a foodie, I am always open to trying new things.

Of course, there will be things, like deep-fried bugs, that I may never want to try. I have enjoyed watching so many TV food shows that imagination had grown, making more adventure, to try new things.

I often like going to the Preston Market, where the energy is more European than Asian. The Oakleigh Market is more Greek-like but very tiny, and I still want to go every now and then as a reminder of my time in Greece.

Where I ate with my eyes and drank in the scenery with breathtaking, picturesque views of the Mediterranean.

I spent a lot of my savings on authentic and artistic gifts that I had to post home, which included many pieces of different carpets in different sizes and lots of jewellery. Also, posting everything back was not a cheap or easy task. Now many souvenirs are poorly made in the east. It's probably much harder to find real, traditional handmade souvenirs. And the price of inflation to factor in is something out of this world.

There was a joke that I could have set up a small shop to display my wares from all the stuff I brought home. On reflection, it wasn't a bad idea, as I would have hauled much, and it would have been so much easier after my return when I decided to uproot and visit more countries.

LOVE AND NEW UNDERSTANDINGS

I first came across the name Kata Tjuta (pronounced ka-tuh joo-tuh) in 1974 on my first visit to the west coast of the South Island, New Zealand. The locals referred to it as Fox River as that's the name used on the map.

I was passing Kata Tjuta on the way to see Roger's sister and brother-in-law's farm and after 40-something years, I connected the name to my experience in Australia with Uluru, the spectacular red tourist spot.

At that time, I was only planning to say goodbye to Roger and leave the country. Travelling across the world to be a devotee to my Indian guru and live in an ashram (spiritual temple) in a foreign land.

So, I was exploring an adventure of new love, my first love.

There was a national newspaper that was known for exaggerating the truth, fabricating headlines to sell more papers—twisted little facts, but in reality, only lies. It was the then popular gossip newspaper than was often far from the truth. More like fabricated lies.

The newspaper headline read: *Lovechild Buried at the Hippy Commune at Fox River.* Maybe it could have read: *Sadly, the Baby Didn't Survive After Birth Due to a Hole in His Heart.*

The story I heard was that the baby was born with a hole in his heart. While still in the womb, his heart was able to beat because of his mother's, but after the cord was cut, his heart was unable to beat on its own. Unfortunately, it was not diagnosed before she gave birth. The death of a child at any age is a terrible loss.

At the time, I didn't know anybody at Kata Tjuta, but over time, things changed. Friendship seeds were sown. Somewhat like my experience of learning how to grow a garden. Not for pretty flowers but for growing food to survive.

These people would quickly become terrific friends and the foundation for my journey into adulthood. They were a vast group of people that I'm still in touch with as I write this. We were a large open community that expanded for miles.

LOVE AND NEW UNDERSTANDINGS

I was an extra in a New Zealand-made movie called *Wild Man*, where you see a very quick flash of me for a second or two. The setting was at Kata-Tjuta/Fox River. You can see the dome, the railway carriage, the latter, the scene and backdrop, and the true West Coast weather, wet, so we were walking around in mud. The movie featured Bruno Lawrence from the band *Blerta* which was famous in those days. Corban Simpson was the lead singer. The cast was not just playing being drunk, they were drunk on cheap wine that cost 25 cents a bottle. With their hand covering the label in all the scenes. Lucky the bottle was brown.

Many of the scriptwriters and the producer went on to make *Goodbye Pork Pie* an iconic famous movie.

With a journey of almost 18 years living there, a few of the people I was familiar with became special lifetime friends; some left and some passed away. Since leaving, I have many memories I reflect on frequently.

The Fox River Glassworks was where I learnt how to blow glass—that was hot stuff! Lyn became Svarama; I can still remember his long flowing hair and beard. He was the first hippy stoner I met at Fox River legend, one of The original settler was Lyn, Savrama, who brought the land for 4000 pounds well over fifty years ago. Many drifters made their home there in those days, some stayed and built their own homes, and others left for new horizons.

One friendship that grew over time was my relationship with Rene. We initially met at a party back in our old hometown. Rene was one of my girlfriends from my hippy days—my happy days! She soon moved to the commune—a community/group of people who share communal land and houses down the road and began a romance with a man who would become Roger's best friend and workmate.

Rene met Bill at Kata Tjuta. Bill was a shearer and lover of horses, particularly Clydesdales, a large and stocky breed of working horses.

Bill rigged a wagon and covered it in the style of the old wild west cowboys, carrying all their gear and provisions with their dog in tow. He took Rene on a camping trip where love and romance blossomed between them. Their love story could be a classic 'Mills and Boon' romance story.

As we both grew up in Wellington, Rene and I would also visit each other's parents and take parcels for them on our separate trips. Some of the things we would send were gifts of fresh produce, something they all loved very much.

I can remember Rene had a shocking habit of lifting *every* lid of *every* pot I had cooking on the coal range out of curiosity. I had to train her not to do that as often as I needed the cover to keep the steam in for the cooking process. So, I would leave little notes saying, 'don't touch.'

Sometimes I would leave a plate of cooked food that got pushed back in the lower warming drawer, totally forgotten about until after the guests left, after the meal.

From this, one can guess we had plenty of food. Thus began my reputation as a pretty good cook, my passion growing from my love of food. Eating and being a bit of a recipe detective, I began to explore. I never liked to measure; I improvised with what ingredients I had. We were around a one-hour drive from the nearest town, so we would only go every four or six weeks unless it was necessary to go into town outside of the time we normally would. If we needed something urgently, we would borrow it from the neighbours at Fox River, Kata Tjuta.

Then came the time when Bill and Rene left.

When they moved to a remote part of the country on the coast, the only access was to walk during the low tide, where they had a wind power system. My request was if I was going to visit and cook, I had to have my ingredients carried in for me as the walk around the coastline was difficult enough, with the receding tide, and walking on the rocks. Apparently one visitor slipped and broke her ankle, she had to be air-lifted out.

It was a hard life. So hard that, in the end, it was better for them to return to the city. I remember a major issue for Rene was that home-schooling didn't offer her boys enough opportunities.

That was often the case. It was from that incredible home living off the grid that these boys developed their musical talents, and they ended up playing music in different countries.

My realisation of Kata Tjuta was singing with the Choir of Hard Knocks when I went there. I finally made that connection, but the earth was not red and dry on the farm back in New Zealand.

For our 10th anniversary, the Choir of Hard Knocks performed in Uluru, also known as Kata Tjuta. The "penny dropped". This spelling was on my fridge magnet and as far as I know, nobody from the old West Coast commune refers about this connection...that I know of, at least. I would really like to find out who named the commune Kata Tjuta. The way it's spelled makes the pronunciation easier. Not being in contact with the original people who started the commune of Kata Tjuta is hard for me to have anything *confirmed*. For me to make that realisation has been of tribal significance of the connection of the term across the ditch related to New Zealand and Australia. My guess is whoever named it initially knew about this, maybe some of the earth was red, or maybe there was an indigenous connection? Perhaps I can continue to do the research to find a deeper meaning and connection.

COOKING IN GREECE

Coming back from my Greek adventure, which was well over 20 years ago. It's a place I have longed to return to since, I'm recalling many treasured memories that have felt a little like reliving that experience from the comfort of my home…it has been interesting. This story is of when I was staying in a rooming house in Mytilene, the capital of Lesvos, where the best ouzo—the national drink of Greece—is made. I missed the hands-on experience of cooking for myself when I was travelling.

In the back of the rooming house, there was a little shed with a couple of small, portable gas camping burners. This was great because I really felt like a change from eating in a restaurant and enjoyed the outcome of my own labour. For me, especially at that time, not cooking for an extended period felt like a withdrawal. Cooking again gave me enjoyment and fun. I had been eating two or three meals out daily for what seemed like weeks and weeks. Some dishes really oozed oil, so I wanted something really simple and plain, which was soul-satisfying. It was fun checking out the local stall where items seemed so cheap; that was another element of a smaller within the bigger adventure.

I bought a few little items like spaghetti, olive oil, tomatoes, olives, cucumber, and a bit of fresh feta. It was like nothing I had ever tasted in the supermarkets back home; there was no comparison. It was home away from home. I made a Greek salad, boiled the pasta, and even found a glass jar of homemade tomato pasta sauce with herbs.

I remember it was still early in the morning before it got hot from the heat of the midday sun, and it seemed like the cooking took quite a while. I also remember taking a photo of this meal as I felt so proud to have put it all together. The only time I cooked for others on this trip was when I was in Thessaloniki. I met some people on the beach who invited me to visit their hometown, where neighbours of the new friends I made turned up over a few nights to taste my cooking. They never showed up empty-handed and always brought a contribution to share, like loaves and fish. These were the people I met on the beach who invited me halfway across Greece to visit them. And being the spontaneously adventurous person I am, I did it at the drop of a hat.

My friends wanted me to stay and start a Chinese cooking school. At the time, I considered it to be a part of my future and I wanted to retire there. I often make impulsive decisions that fizzle out and I had not put any planning into it. While I do long to go back, I know I'll never be able to relive the old experiences, as it will be a new and fresh adventure, when and if it happens.

SANCTUARY

I am typing and composing, a new way of writing, and building up confidence with this.

This story is about my good friend Andrea and her husband Nelson. Nelson is a devotee of Hari Krishna, while Andrea is not. Andrea is a fantastic artist. These are things I want to note at the beginning of this story.

When I stay with them, I spend time attending chanting meetings with Nelson. Andrea and I create art together and go swimming in the sea.

Andrea has made each bedroom in their cottage sea-themed. I stayed in the grandchildren's bedroom, the fairy room. One whole wall had been colourfully painted, from the ceiling to the floor. The other room had a sea theme with mermaids and seahorses.

I met Andrea at art school where we clicked right away. She's an amazing, creative, spirited, and wild woman. She lives her life unselfishly in devotion to others her loved ones and cares for animals of all kinds.

Starting with her family and her extended heart in her love for so many living beings. She embraces me as a sister from another mother. I knew her mother, a famous psychic who I went to many times before we realised there was a connection. Wellington is a very small city with less than six degrees of separation. Her pets are an extension of her; they're a part of who she is. Her home, her house, never has a lock on it. The door is always open. So, in fact, it's the most open house/home I have ever come across that's literally a living vibration of the title, true to the words. Her door is open to all, but they had to start locking their home after a burglary.

She's also my soul sister.

I have many soul connections, both her and Nelson are my soul family. I find these connections stronger than my blood family.

Her being there for me when I most needed a friend, especially when I felt a little lost without a home when I was torn between my love for two countries, Australia and New Zealand, is something I'll always hold dear to me.

SANCTUARY

Having a friend like her is a gift, a godsend, and for those of you readers, my future friends whom I have yet to meet. If you have a friend that fits this profile, I know you'll understand my meaning. Sometimes I feel she runs an orphanage for all living beings. She has an extensive collection of pets, from a cockatoo named Ipo, who is her oldest pet of over 30 years and the kingpin of the house, and a small magpie with a broken wing, called Negro, who lives in a cage, mainly for his own protection, from other, animals, especially cats.

She's so house proud. When her housework is done, and all the pets are outside, I swear the floors are clean enough to eat off. She keeps her house, her home, immaculately clean and tidy. She has a touch for magical design and artistic talents that can transform visitors in her home. A fantastical journey when one enters her life, her home, an Aladdin's cave, and a fairy house. No, I'm not just saying fairy-like house, it's honestly is a sanctuary to me; my second home. It's not just things that make a home but the love of the people living there.

When I come here, I feel as though I am in *Neverland*. It has been many forms of heaven for me, not just a roof over my head, but a shelter from the storm. No matter what the weather outside is, being here for me is a retreat. It's a safe place that nourishes not only my spirit and soul, but a home from the storms of the battles we face daily, even when the sun might not be shining so solid and bright. There was a beautiful hanging mirror at my hip level, at eye level, for the kids to see their own reflection, amazing that was so well thought out.

Walking out of the house, down a small driveway, across the road to the sea, walking onto pebbles, driftwood, and sand. It's a treasured landscape for any beachcomber.

Being here I always forget all my pros and cons that word to the phrase often used 'No worries, man,' but in this case, 'no worries, *women.*'

It's by far more homely to me than any home I have ever owned, rented, or stayed in. I listen to the quiet chorus of seagulls, and the roar of the planes flying past. The morning bells of the local birds and the birds that are in and out, the ones in nature and the ones in the cage, chirping away.

Ipo, her beloved cockatoo, was given to her many, many years ago. I have calculated Ipo's bird years as a senior, well over a couple of hundred years old, equal to human years as one year of a cockatoo is equal to nine or ten human years. Due to his health and skin allergies, Ipo wears ponchos that often match Andrea's dresses that she has made for herself, using the leftover fabric for Ipo. She prefers to call them ponchos rather than dresses, as Ipo is male. Andrea has an eccentric fashion sense. Pictures of them wearing matching outfits are often featured in the local newspapers.

SANCTUARY

Her garden is a graveyard of her beloved dogs that have passed. With the passing of a beloved dog, she would always take in another or adopt from someone that could no longer look after their own dog. She and her husband have lived in their home for decades, raising their children there that have long flown the nest, with some flying back to the home when they're in between periods of having their own home. The grandchildren come to stay, and the children's bedrooms are decorated with the most amazing painted walls. Some of them are life-like papier-mache art, of a fish and a lion's face that's straight out of the jungle book, and the head of a life-size donkey. Originally, it was life-sized, but after the body broke, Andrea recreated its head, like how a hunter mounts the game he has killed. There's a painted feature wall full of fairies, unicorns, and a magical castle. The room is an artist's heaven and a child's delight. It's an enchanted wonderland.

Hanging on the wall beside the door is a gold-framed, beautifully clear mirror that is perfectly clean. I see reflections of the artwork depending on what angle I am sitting or lying. Yes, this magical mirror is hung at such a low level that it makes me feel like a giant when I bend to see into a Tom Thumbs-size mirror for tiny children to use and enjoy. It's so practical and well thought of to have it at this height, but probably rarely done with small children in mind. It also had a rack of dress-ups, and playhouses, all of them delightfully decorated.

The adult in me enjoyed being in the fairy room; one whole wall was painted with fairies and castles, and unicorns. The bigger room (the mermaid room) was already occupied, the child in me was so deliciously excited that I got to sleep in the children's room. I shared with her granddaughter Rosie when she came to stay overnight. Rosie was around the age of four or five at the time, and during her visit, we read books and had tea parties with a ceramic tea set I recognised from my childhood. I gave it to her grand-daughter, now a teenager. I loved my time there; it was almost two months on that visit as I couldn't decide which country, I wanted to call home next. What helped me make that decision was I missed my singing and the choir back in Melbourne.

I only have a small group of special friends that have lasted a lifetime. They are my chosen family. With memorable moments and valued times, strumming on a ukulele and singing into the wee hours, sitting around a wood fire. Yes, I can remember all this very well; it's my second home.

My soul sister friendship with Andrea is my experience of this moment etched in my soul like a treasured tattoo.

THE PERFECT GIFT

T he first Christmas with my Italian, Chinese, and British grandson.

I travelled far, to a different hemisphere, to winter across the other side of the world. Forgoing my summer at home.

So, for some months before, I collected bits and pieces for his stocking. What would I get for an 18-month-old boy?

I pondered this for a few months prior. I went to different toy shops before I came across a small local stationery shop with two things inside that stood out. One was a small tepee, and the other a wooden train set. I chose the latter as it was small and compact rather than big. The tepee had wooden poles to form the support for the canvas of the tepee, so it was quite large.

My suitcase was full of big and small gifts for him and treats for my family in the UK and the Italian side coming together. Tim Tams, Cherry Ripes, and BBQ Shapes for extended family too.

This train set's wooden tracks extended to a meter and a half, with small figurines, signals, signs, bridges, the combination of the front engine, two carriages and a caboose, each having a small magnetic dome button front and back, except the very front of the engine and the last carriage. The train could be tolled and hand-guided along the track, with all the carriages and caboose in sequence.

The magnetic connections curved around to glide along the tracks smoothly. All the family and friends that saw him with it played with him continually. They all praised my choice of such a spot-on present.

This gift remained his absolute favourite for a few years, even after receiving more elaborate and fancy train sets with batteries. Some of the tracks were well over a square meter laid out on the carpet when set up. He got swift and set them up by himself.

This gift started his passion for Thomas the Tank Engine. My grandson even knows the name of all his fire engine friends. From around two years old, he quickly remembered all the characters from *Thomas and Friends*.

THE PERFECT GIFT

The trains are still growing and accumulating gifts from his fifth and sixth birthdays.

I need to rattle my brains for a fantastic gift for his seventh birthday coming up soon. The question is, what will be his future interests, still trains? Especially *Thomas and Friends*? There could be a lot of letting go with some of his current toy collection to fit in what he'll be given for Christmas.

COVID BIRTHDAY BLUES

This Covid-19 pandemic has been an enjoyable, introspective time where I had no outward distractions. I developed a new and more profound improvement in my relationship with moi/myself.

I discovered a sort of *Jekyll and Hyde* inside of me.

Isolation has been a time of incubation for my new inner self to emerge. It's been my personal time to dwell and spend time in the inner cave of my thoughts. Learn more about my inner self without distraction from going out in the world. In a way, it's been somewhat like letting a part of my old self die, then being able to rise` from the ashes of the fire like a phoenix.

I've been finding the balance between daily exercise and movement. Venturing out for daily walks to the nearest supermarket. Firstly, to get me out and exercise, and secondly, to catch bargains. My freezer was filled to the brim, cooking up a storm and eating for me and myself as if I was cooking for someone else. That was the new me I would unfold over the months as I evolved with the circumstances.

I had a solo party on Zoom on the first of the two birthdays in lockdown to connect with my loved ones and friends. I asked friends to share a story, poem, or song.

On the first birthday lockdown, I arranged a Zoom party with my friends from all around Australia.

My friend Suzy and my spiritual teacher managed to deliver and planned a special treat after the serenade of a handsome guitar strumming from Cliff.

The delivery of a giant platter of seafood, from cooked prawns, mussels, opened oysters, and even a most unusual type of roe called kina, took me by surprise.

My second birthday in lockdown wasn't as memorable. There was no Zoom party this year, just a few calls and loads of messages on Facebook, the delivery of an Italian gourmet box of goodies full of all sorts of truffle products, from my Italian family. And with no Zoom party, it was a much quieter day of self-entertainment in my animal print pyjamas, singing karaoke on my smart TV, singing my lockdown blues, and feasting on my truffle box of goodies. I love truffle mushrooms.

I was all by my lonesome self with technology to chat. My living room was filled with voices without paying for toll calls. There are no charges other than having a good internet service. I feel as if this has been, in a way, a saving grace. With zoom meetings all over the world. The best and most unusual birthday party was the virtual party with the enormous seafood platter.

A feast for one! I might have put on a few kilos, but it was no big deal. Summertime was approaching, and with that came the freedom to explore new ways to feel fitter. The region was my muse, and I was longing to return to the new normal, whatever that might be. Then there was the 5 km rule—only being allowed to leave up to 5 km from my place of residence. The long and short of Covid-19 was that the benefits outweighed the lockdown blues, for me.

Plus, some of the extra benefits lockdown had given me were more time alone and the courage to explore who I am.

Things have been far from natural in the last couple of years since Covid-19 fired up. I was a mixture of neither happy nor sad, and some days I felt like I was in limbo. It's not accurate or unreal, but a true sense of contentment with everything as it was far from the life I lived before.

I was ready to spend time doing stuff I hadn't made time for pre-lockdown. It felt like the start of a new relationship, falling in love again and getting to know me, learning more about me. Also, getting to like and love myself with more depth and understanding of the idea that was developing and growing with a sense of utter excitement. Somewhat like how I have felt each time in the past, when I started to feel an attraction to someone, the joy, the blushing, and the butterflies without that old stress and worry of if it's the right thing. It was a fabulous and completely brand-new sensation. It felt naturally good no longer coming from fear as I was about to venture into something new. It almost felt like an attraction toward a special new romance with myself.

I may never lose myself again, but this time it wasn't outwardly, it was inwardly. Knowing and owning my new feelings brought up a happy burst of contentment and energy that turned into a deeply empowering feeling.

It felt like I had time to re-value who I am, who I was, and who I would like to become. A comfortable new sensation and it was beginning to feel like the birth of the latest and improved version, a bolder and stronger woman than I was that, and that I was finally becoming. There's a song I remembered from an old movie called *getting to know you, getting to know (Musical-The King and I)*.

COVID BIRTHDAY BLUES

I found that I preferred being at home, zooming in on meetings, and learning new things. Doing only things I wanted when I wanted. From eating and sleeping to watching movies all day, if that's what I felt like. In the beginning, it was like I wasn't entirely alone. If the television was on, I could choose the company and allocate how I spent my time. I started to follow the series that expanded my mind, and movies that not only made me laugh but had me talking to myself as well.

Having nobody to report back to also meant having a sense of freedom; I had no one telling me what to do. I sang, laughed, and cried at times as well, all to pass the time away, hour by hour, day by day, month by month... that was for almost two years. The gift from the universe was I newfound joy and richness within myself. Was... joyful, rich, a gift...

I was invited to join the board for senior housing, I was excited and chuffed, still nine months down the track. In the past, pre-lockdown, most days, I would be rushing off to catch trains and buses and going to the gym to get fit. I'm so laid back these days that I sometimes have difficulty venturing out to see people. Doing anything that was part of my old norm takes considerable effort. In some ways, I feel shy and prefer my own company over others. So, I'm not the extrovert I used to be and now I'm more introverted.

SELF-ABSORPTION TO SELF AWARENESS

I've realised the difference between thinking and feeling. There's self-realisation in seeing the situation through my own interpretation and the outside view of the real, actual situation. Inside eyes and outside eyes.

Myths and truths—thinking isn't knowing. Thinking about yourself doesn't mean you know yourself. That was a big lightbulb moment for me. For instance, I love to holiday and think about it all the time, but unless I do the research, I'll never get going.

Introspection/Self Realisation = Self Examination.

In the past, I have done a lot of introspection. For me now, that seems just like taking the first steps. When we reach self-realisation and then examine, we come to another level of understanding on yet another step of the ladder to our achievement of *self*. How do we choose the right approach? Do we take others' points of view to embrace them as our own, or do we seek our own personal views and own them?

Psychoanalyse ourselves/seek therapy? Adopting a flexible mindset, I've always asked the 'why' question as an exploration. Self-therapy from regular meditation can be an important part of looking after ourselves. Having a professional to talk to can get a lot of burden off our chest.

I've been examining the cause of my thoughts, feelings, and behaviours, often searching for the answer.

Asking *what* instead of *why* makes me investigate what My emotions and around it.

That's why I have found that keeping a journal is voicing my feelings to myself at the time I write it, and when I re-read it, my emotions are no longer in the same space.

Expressive writing can provide a powerful direction in self-discovery, seeing both sides, the positive and the negative.

Even if it's only for a short time, beginning with five minutes then extending to fifteen, and growing to thirty minutes. Writing has become easier the more I write.

HUNTING AND GATHERING

I like to pop into my local supermarket on a Monday morning shortly after opening. Other mornings are good too, but I have found Mondays are best. My local supermarket is only a five-minute walk away. Some Mondays it's an effort, but mostly it's a real saving that helps keep my budget down, so it's worth it.

Yesterday I decided to get myself ready to leave early to search for bargains but there was nothing there.

The following day I went early again and returned home with some great specials.

I chose a meat pack containing three pieces of Chicken Maryland, which is a cut we have here that's made up of the drumstick and the thigh together. Therefore, each piece is a reasonably good size, with three of them weighing a bit over 1.5kg. That's three good-sized meals.

Each piece can become two meals, so the total is up to at least six meals. This is another reminder that sometimes, it's good to be flexible with no planned menu.

I have found these meats are only sold cheaply if the use-by date is coming up or if I buy them on the use-by day. I try to cook it all on the same day, but often there are a least three days to use them up. I also try to marinate them as soon as possible, which helps to flavour and tenderise the meat. This is something I either do as soon as I get home or later that day. Sometimes, I will freeze it as soon as I get home.

In this case, I was out, but after dinner, I rubbed each piece with a different flavour. I can then cook them all at once and freeze them or freeze them all if I don't have the time to marinate and cook them straight away. The freezing enhances the flavours more than just cooking it as it is. I learnt from an ex-housemate from Vietnam, who just boiled it for a specific time according to the size of each portion. Then he makes a quick salad and uses the Vietnamese salad dressing for both the chicken and the salad. It certainly makes for a super quick meal with virtually no preparations. In the case of my three pieces of Marland Chicken, I found the meat so tasty I often use the meat eaten off the bones to make some stock that could be used for another one of my no-fuss quick recipes. For example, a noodle soup dish. I often make the stock and freeze that for my noodle soup I have a good stock straight out of freezer. A tasty base for my soups.

One of the past cooking classes I taught at night for adult education was titled *Budget Cooking on a Shoestring*, which was so popular for the entire time it ran until I left the country. I, for one, don't like to eat the same meal more than twice a week. So, it's a matter of thinking on my feet, planning the meal as I go, when I see what's on sale or on special, I make that choice as I go along. I take the time to prepare the meat and the cooking. The same applies to the vegetables I buy. I think on the spot to work out if I have the time and the energy to process them, before buying.

In the past, I have called this *Hunting and Gathering*, which is my play on words. The hunting is going to the local market and shop, unlike the caveman meaning of this. Going out to source food, or gather it, is my take on describing my shopping technique. Hunting and gathering, a term I use in looking out for bargains.

This way of thinking and preparing saves me a lot of time preparing and cooking. It's ideal, not only for families but for the singles that are budgeting. Also, being time-poor is common for most people these days. Menu planning comes afterwards for this process, which is opposite to many people who often choose a menu, then make a shopping list. I like doing it my way best as it adds to the element of fun, but it's also using what is readily available and in season. Avoid paying higher prices for food out of season.

It's my playing with words, hunting and shopping, finding the bargain.

TIME FOR A RECIPE

TOASTED SEEDS

Fast recipe for a super tasty condiment!

This is a very quick and simple recipe that can be made in minutes.

Half cup of the sesame seeds—I use a 1/4 cup each of white and black (great contrast of colour).

Pink Himalayan sea salt—give about 15 twists on a salt grinder, around a teaspoon.

Use a heavy bottom pan.

First, put seeds in the cold pan, and heat them on med-high for a few minutes.

Depending on the heat source, gas or electricity, this toasting takes two to three minutes, so keep a close watch, and toss the seeds or use a wooden spoon.

Turn off the heat if the seeds look toasted enough, then remove the pan from the heat but leave the seeds in the pan—they'll continue toasting with the residual heat.

Add in the salt, use a little less or more according to taste, and then use a heavy-based glass to crush the Seeds with and blend with the salt. Mortar and pestle if you have one. When cooled down, store in an airtight jar.

I call it my magical sprinkles and use it on any dish, especially on salads or even on my tomato sandwiches as it adds a fantastic taste to everything. It can also be used as table salt, and it keeps for months…but mine gets used up too fast to be kept that long.

TIPS AND TRICKS

This short story is me sharing a few basic tips and tricks that I use and hope you'll find them particularly helpful.

I decided a long time ago that if I couldn't grow my vegetables, not being able afford buying organic, I would investigate ways to upgrade the quality of what I brought cheap with whatever method in exploring how to improve them. Using AVC (apple cider vinegar) Around a teaspoon in bowl of water. Use more for bigger amounts of produce and more water.

I would have a bowl large enough to hold vegetables or even use the kitchen sink for a big bunch of silver beet. Using, a small container of blueberries. Put them in cold water to cover the berries, add a couple of teaspoons of apple cider vinegar, and soak for at least 15 to 20 minutes.

Don't soak longer than 20mins, half a hour- as the goodness will start to steep out of the fruit and vegetables. The AVC can clean sprays and pesticides, but not much longer than half an hour, as the goodness of the produce will start steeping out.

I go to the fresh wet markets about an hour before closing. I have a quick walk around, never stopping to buy the first thing I see that looks good because when I do, I end up seeing something better later. Especially even better quality and better bargains.

I was shown that baking soda can be used to tenderise meat but be very careful not to use too much for a quick fix. With tough cuts of meat, I've found this can leave a residue taste, if too much is used.

But I've used a little baking soda in my marinades for meat, as my mother taught me, but not too much as too many changes the flavour, which I just don't like.

It's amazing how it can tenderise meat quickly and helps in the cleaning of vegetables. But I still prefer using a few teaspoons of apple cider vinegar for vegetables.

As many markets have days they're closed for business, like Victoria market on Mondays and Tuesdays. Seafood and meat reductions happen drastically the day before a public holiday, sometimes down to half price. But now with the cost of living constantly rising, they seem to not be giving food away as cheaply as it was a few years back.

Those days, I could get a $1 bag of ripe fruit and vegetables but buying cheap produce like this means they must be used fast, within a day or two at the most as they won't keep as long as buying the fresh new produce. This is a good time to buy but only if you have the time to cook or freeze, it easily becomes waste if I don't make the time or find time to process it, cooking of freezing.

I often like to make jams, pickles, marmalade, and chutney, especially for gifts at Christmas time. If you do this or would like to, I can assure you how simple it can be to do so. A little planning ahead to have jars on standby is a great start, and it means being prepared. I know from past experience, I have tried to rush out to buy jars at the last minute, only to find it hard to find the right size–not too small, not too big, but the most suitable in presentation.

I feel like it's an expression from my heart that I care to put my time into them. Giving a homemade gift shows thought and time.

Target or Kmart often have boxes of jars with lids for spices and herbs. Suitable for storing your homemade sauces, jams, chutneys, etc. Sometimes they sell very cheaply, but never when you need them, so it's better to be prepared.

During the week in mid-afternoons, produce is often reduced at my local IGA. But be careful, they might raise the price and then reduce it to make it seem like a bargain. My local IGA also offers 5% off for pensioners on Thursdays.

During lockdown, some clothing shops like Dimmeys, a local clothing store, in Braybrook got smart and started selling food to fit the category to remain open. Seniors have a 5% off on Wednesday on showing a senior's card, not a pension card.

I often buy meat on special to slice and cut up for a lower price as the labour and time involved increases the cost so much more. Meat that's sliced and prepared for use can double the price I've noticed. So only buy if you're time-poor. I've lived in a place without refrigeration and had to learn to preserve food out of necessity. I have the time and plus the know-how, to do all the prep involved. In cutting and slicing, marinating then freezing, so it can keep for longer, especially if I don't have the time to use and cook it by its use-by date, I prepare and freeze it. Once it's defrosted, it's ready to cook and eat, without needed to cut it, or slice it. On busy days when I'm away from home most of the day, I take a package out of the freezer to defrost. Pre-prepared and seasoned portions are ready for cooking as soon as I walk in the door, so it takes away the cutting and the marinating time to cook from scratch and the meat has more time to take on the marinated flavours while it's frozen.

TIPS AND TRICKS

For homemade dumplings, I often make double the mix and freeze one lot so I'll have some ready to go for next time without all the prep.

Always have a spare carry bag in your bag to save having to pay for a new one every time you go out.

A tiny bit of baking soda sprinkled over pieces of *tough cuts*, tenderise the meat. But be careful not to overdo this, as it can change the taste to a slight bitterness.

Investigate the price reduction time at your local grocery.

Seniors have a discount in certain shops. My local Dimmeys, another version of Kmart and Target, has 5% off on Wednesdays, but they need to view your seniors' card.

Baking soda with hot water to soak burnt pots makes cleaning easier.

Buying dried herbs and spices is better in small amounts to keep the actual flavour. Sitting around for long periods, they lose their zing. So, unless you're cooking for large crowds, events, or hospitality, avoid thinking it's a saving buying in large amounts to have them sitting around and losing the goodness.

I've found an air fryer is a much healthier way to enjoy crispy fried food without all the deep-fried oil. I can't live without an air fryer in my kitchen. I have a drawer-style one, plus an oven-style one. They each have different capacities and qualities in cooking to give quicker and tastier results. Enjoying healthier fried food with little to no oil is much better for us. Plus, fewer calories.

They've saved me so much time and can be even quicker than buying takeout or eating out. It's especially so much healthier knowing all the ingredients in your food and no extra flavour enhancers and other additives that aren't even mentioned in your takeout. Things like MSG can upset stomachs, create horrible dryness, and cause headaches, just to name a few side effects. Monosodium glutamate, a flavour enhancer, is not a natural product. I always check the label when buying new produce.

It comes back to back to what you were brought up with. For example, one of my older friends. My best friend's mum. I would pop in when her daughter was away for work, I would ring and ask what she felt like so I could pick up a takeaway to share some 25 years ago, and she would always ask me to go places that she knew used MSG, she seemed to enjoy it so much more than me with no side effects at all. I guess her body was so used to it.

Nowdays, even with more awareness regarding food and additives, the choice is still a very personal one for individuals.

CHINESE DUMPLINGS

1. Chicken Dumplings
2. Gyoza
3. Potstickers
4. Xiaolongbao

The traditional dumpling is a single bite with a few ingredients, served as a snack or as a main. That's why yum cha is about a selection of various little bites. Also, it's traditional to share—the more people, the more food is presented.

With origins dating back to ancient China, most big groups can sit ten people around a circular table. It makes using a *Lazy Susan* in the centre very convenient. With a touch of a finger, what was hard to reach was turned in whatever direction. For guests at the other end of the table, it's easy to move the food in front for easy access. Little dough balls flattened out to carry many delicious little parcels of meat, seafood, and vegetables.

The skins/wrappers to make dumplings are sold readily in stores, even the local supermarket, now.

In the past, they had to be homemade or purchased in an Asian store. It's easy to make. You can get them thin with a lot of rolling or by using a pasta machine to roll them.

Here's a basic recipe for dumpling wrappers/skins to try if you can make the time:

Four cups of flour (there's a special dumpling flour) to one cup of water. Then you mix them in a large bowl (I use chopsticks to mix). And note, it's best made the day before consumption.

Variations: rice or tapioca, which are gluten-free.

Wrappers/skins are mainly made from wheat, as you can often see a dusting of flour.

CHICKEN DUMPLINGS

If chicken mince is difficult to find, I make my own chicken dumplings by using dark meat, such as the thighs, not the breast. I grind the meat in a food processor—ideal

CHINESE DUMPLINGS

for steaming, pan-frying, or deep-frying. My tip is that the longer the marinating time, the juicier the taste. I double or divide it in half for this mix, and then freeze one portion so it reduces the preparation time considerably, for the next time.

500 grams of chicken mince
Small can of water chestnuts or bamboo shoots
2 teaspoon sesame oil
2 teaspoon soy sauce
Around an inch of fresh ginger root, finely grated
3 green spring onions finely chopped
½ teaspoon white pepper
1 and a half tablespoon salt
1 tablespoon sugar
¾ cup (1 small) grated carrot
1 tablespoon Shaoxing wine
2 tablespoon hoisin sauce
Around 1 and ½ cups of finely shredded wombok (Chinese cabbage)
Mix all this and leave overnight in the fridge.
If in a hurry marinate the ingredients at least an hour before wrapping, longer or overnight is even better and tastier.

CRAVINGS

Cravings for certain foods bring back memories of the person I enjoyed the meals with.

For the last few days, I've had an intense craving for nachos, which I've never had a craving for before, so it took me a few days to source the ingredients I needed. My craving is normally noodle soup, a comfort food that I have regularly. In the past, I have denied myself as I knew it wasn't healthy. If it's homemade, it can make it much better. I grew up on instant noodles as we didn't know any better then.

Even with teaching cooking for over 30 years, I've never felt like making nachos or even ordering it when eating out. I would Google the recipe for anything I had never made before and wanted to try, then adjust it to suit the ingredients I had on hand.

It was the only dish my Airbnb guest Michael could confidently make, something I had forgotten, I used to eat out many years ago, as snack food in a bar the version he made for me.

I've probably eaten this dish a few times, so I Googled the recipe. It's my fallback, researching recipes I want to have a go at. I also tend to tweak the recipe a little as I'm not even sure how Michael made his version, and his had at least four times the amount of cheese, making it incredibly rich. I realised this while I was munching on corn chips, memories of Michael, flashes back. He was like a lost boy whom I felt maternal with as he was a year older than my eldest child. I call him a boy as he was about a year older than my eldest child.

He arrived to live with me via Airbnb with an extensive list of food requirements, and I found, I liked cooking for people, as it was a big challenge to cater to him. I love challenges. Maybe it was the mother in me. His birthday is the same as my grandson's, and he wanted to celebrate it by inviting me out to dinner a few days After he arrived. I was touched by his awareness and consideration.

While he was living with me, he had a secret wish he didn't want to share in case he *jinxed* it. His dream was to go to America to study acting and make it in New York.

All this happened some years ago, and he has not come into my mind until today as I was eating one of the few dishes he had mastered, nachos.

We built a good friendship, watched DVDs, and shared many spiritual views, but his ideas were more set-in concrete. He came from a mixed-race background, much like my own children. His opinions were as strict as his father's, who ruled with a fist of iron. My heart ached from some of his stories as he still carried years of pain and went to therapy. It was so interesting; he said nobody had ever been able to cater for him, so I made it my goal and challenge to do so.

He said he didn't know what he wanted but had just returned from travelling. I remember he came *back* to a cosy government job after his travels that was kept open for him. In many ways, he was very considerate as he took me out for dinner often as a thank you for cooking daily for him. He had a daily ritual breakfast and lunch that he ate at the office, so to have a surprise dinner catering to his dietary needs as a form of love and nurturing he had never received in any condition was something he was grateful for. I think his most extended relationships never reached a double figure in the form of a few months. But in other ways, he was tough and stubborn; this was something I learnt after a short time. As a mother, I enjoyed having someone to care for.

Towards the end of his stay, he became moody and told me to stop cooking for him. Shortly after, he shared the happy news of his green card and gave me, notice, and said he was going to stop all his social media accounts, emails, phone contact, etc, as his way of wiping away his existence. I remember his anger for his parents was still weighing heavy, so I'm sure he never said goodbye to them.

What inspired me to write this about him came so suddenly. It was my craving to taste something he reintroduced me to—nachos.

He was a stranger who became a friend quickly but is now no longer a friend. I believe he's currently somewhere in the USA. I send love and health, and sometimes say a prayer for him from time to time. In some ways, on another level, he was almost like the son I never had. Living a year together as adults was something I had never got to experience with my daughters, who left home young.

Something tells me I need to try to tweak this recipe again to try to get an even better-tasting version of it.

I have been to Mexico and didn't ever see nachos on any menu. Food can be like fashion trends, with certain styles coming back into fashion again years later.

BEST COFFEE EVER

After island hopping in Greece, I sailed to Italy and saw the Pope at the Vatican from a distance. He seemed barely two inches high from where I stood. Seeing the Colosseum was amazing, but the true highlight was the first cup of coffee I had standing up at the train station on my arrival in Rome. It costs more sitting down. It took me a little while to understand, as sitting takes more space, cost more.

In those days, I liked my coffee extra strong, and I noticed that people were mainly standing, which seemed to be the preferred way. I found it to be more complicated in Rome as most Italian people didn't seem to understand or speak as much English as they do in Greece. After drinking, I learnt the technique of reading the coffee grounds. A fun form of entertainment and sometimes, it can be accurate. After the coffee is finished, turn the cup three times one way, then another three times the opposite way. Then, quickly turn the cup upside down onto the saucer. Leaving it to drain for a few moments to build the anticipation. I close my eyes and silently ask for permission to be guided To speak my interpretation of the grounds that has formed into a pattern. A symbolic prediction for the future of the drinker of that coffee.

My stay in Rome was in a hostel, which I found in the *Lonely Planet* travel guide, with mixed dorm rooms of up to 20 bunks. Meeting fellow travellers was part of the excitement. The hostel was taking walk-ins long before the days of internet booking or emails. There was normally a mix of dorms in hostels, which was sometimes a little confusing to see which bed was mine in the semi-dark, I quickly learnt to pay a bit more for a smaller dorm of four to six with a toilet.

I spent what seemed like hours at the Rome railway station, being sent from counter to counter trying to buy a ticket on the Eurostar overnight train to France. I was amazed by how calm I was, even though there was a bit of a wait. A smartly dressed man approached me offering money. He might have thought I was soliciting or being the opportunist, offering to take me to see places in poor English; maybe it was a misunderstanding. I was catching local transport—buses and trams—making new friends from different parts of the world with whom I kept in touch for a while. I took the overnight fast train to Paris to the

Louvre Museum to see the Mona Lisa and the Statue of David, created by Michelangelo.

I journeyed to Holland and the Netherlands with the family that hosted my daughter for a one-year in a student exchange program a few years before my travels. They found out it was my birthday, and my host family offered three varieties of birthday cakes. They took me over the border to Germany to a town called Badham. After that, I went to Denmark, where I stayed with a dear friend's parents and had a private guided tour of the crown jewels, from her sister. From there, I caught up with friends in London before flying to Los Angeles to visit my cousin and his family. I went to Disneyland and Universal Studios, and a trip to Las Vegas blew me away in enjoyment. The free shows on the strip were wonderful. I went to San Francisco, Fisherman's Wharf, Bubba Gump Shrimp Co., which was inspired by the seafood from the famous movie *Forrest Gump* where the seafood chowder and lemon-lime pie was to die for.

In Portland, I visited the famous Borders, the bookshop that spans over two blocks. I love books but limit myself from buying too many, as carrying too many would incur an extra cost with it being overweight. I spent two weeks with my mother's cousin Kim recovering from the massive trip before cancelling the last leg to Canada due to exhaustion, missing my own bed, and feeling over living out of a suitcase, in my case, it was a backpack.

MORE THAN ONE MOTHER

I had empathy for how important it was for a young woman to have other mothers in a tribal sense. Sometimes, mother and daughter vibrations are not in tune, and both can be too stubborn to see the situation. Having been there and done that, I can see the bigger picture. The solution, in most cases, is communication. It's the merry-go-round too, around, and around, analysing and processing, keeping it moving and flowing.

Recently, I've been reminiscing about just how many women there have been, and mother figures that gave me Beginning of adolescence my mother, went on a three month holiday that extended to a year. I felt a sense of abandonment. I was never briefed on this. I work through the issues as an adult to be able to accept her actions and release emotions from that experience. One of my daughters had different women who took on mothering roles for her. I did some self awareness with this. I knew and accepted it was good for her and what was needed - if I couldn't be there for her, someone was able to be of I took on the same role to young women, as a mother figured as well. My daughter's best friend called me "mother #2" and I called her my daughter #3.

My mother went on a three-month holiday when I was 13, which ended up being extended for a whole year, and never once did she make contact. My theory was she never took her responsibilities as a mother seriously. Phone calls were very expensive, and even if she wrote, which she didn't do, I couldn't read Chinese characters, but she could have written to my father who didn't pass on the messages.

In the early 1980s, I left my children for around four weeks while I travelled to Hong Kong and China with my mother. I wrote postcards, sent letters, and scheduled a collect call home to speak at least once while I was away.

I watched how women express themselves as mothers. Some are too soft, and some might be too hard. It takes a lot of work to pull ourselves out of the web of deception, to break old patterns. Repeating mothering patterns and making some of the same mistakes as my mother. As a mother, I feel it's up to me to change what I can to mend my relationship with my children. There have been so many books written on this, the famous book, *My Mother, My Self* by Nancy Friday.

I don't feel a need to contribute any more than an acknowledgement in a little short story about how it's essential to consciously not treat my daughters the way I felt I was treated by my own mother. Writing a journal to reflect on feelings that might seem ordinary, but then when I read them, I can see that I may have come from a different place at the time of writing them down, which helps to let feelings go, and release them.

So, a healing suggestion I have learnt is to write things down and then have a ritual of burning the paper, it's written on to let it all go. Yes, letting words burn away in the fire is a good ritual of release.

This is how I deal with things, as it can be different for others.

AFTERWORD

What I learnt from writing my stories has not only taught and shown me how far I've come, but the importance of why I have written them has surfaced and unfolded. In a way, my stories are a part of me that I want to continue sharing, even after I'm gone. My family, my friends, and maybe strangers in the future can celebrate the adventures I have written about and my joy of living. Written words speak without a voice or sound. It's my legacy for the future, and I like to say in writing this book I have made a difference.

The pen to paper, writing everything down, that part was easy compared to the labour-some hours of the birthing and the process of all the editing. Persistence through so many technical issues that came with working on a laptop, the world of technology. Editing was where I spent long hours staying up, like tending to a newborn. A new parent, juggling the process of following instructions and getting everything right.

My first book is my metaphor for giving birth, a mixture of fear and excitement of the unknown yet to come. My plan was to repeat, grow, and contemplate with more hindsight for the next book/birth so I'll be somewhat more prepared from already having the experience. And to bring a sense of harmony from the chaos.

I have experienced surges of learning about myself, my past, and how the process, now, has changed me. Now, I, in writing these words, these after-thoughts, believe, truly…that…I am a writer.

And the silence of words can even make more of an impact than spoken words, at times. Choosing the right word can also help paint a picture and without the use of a colour palette, I learnt how a wrongly spelled word can confuse the story and take it out of context.

The significance of choosing the right words, ones that are understandable. To share the pictures I've already painted for myself in The writing, and sharing of these stories, has been a joy.

ABOUT THE AUTHOR

ChuPing migrated to New Zealand as a six-year-old and commenced primary school without speaking English. After four years at secondary school, she went off to explore the university of life.

What followed was a brief encounter with fashion design which transformed into a love of culinary cuisine informed by impromptu ingredients. This culminates in her holistic view on life as an artist, covering her three passions: wellness, fashion design/art and culinary cuisine. However, this is surpassed by her greatest passion, staying forever young at heart.

Her work becomes play as her motto is, "Life shouldn't be a struggle; if you're not having fun, you're not living right."

ChuPing was a successful massage therapist, often booked out weeks in advance. She also taught adults continuing education cooking classes and self-maintenance at Wellington High, New Zealand.

ChuPing has a broad range of skills from childcare, to cooking, to bus driving, with bundles of life experience to boot.

She is an exhibition artist with experience in an assortment of mediums, as well as certified in peer community education, and a volunteer for hosting Senior's Link Transport day trips.

ACKNOWLEDGEMENTS

I would like to express my deepest gratitude to the following:

My beautiful daughters Ming and Dawn, who are strong young women. I've seen how they have nurtured my grandsons, Antonio and Jordan, who are equally strong. Both my girls have inspired me with their achievements. Not living in the same country, I hold them dear to my heart, as they're my blood family.

The Choir of Hard Knocks ignited my passion for singing, building the endorphins that keep my heart healthy. The founder, Dr. Jonathan Walsh, inspired my heart with song. Matt Jones for his permission to use his spectacular photograph of us at Uluru. My singing family.

My fairy godmother Mary Helen, who opened my mind to crystals. Celebrating her 80th Birthday in Melbourne, where I first heard the choir perform, gave me the inspiration to move countries.

Taking me to the best eateries both in Melbourne and Wellington and to the best Yum-char establishments. Part of my spiritual family in New Zealand.

My friend and spiritual teacher, Suzy Rideout and her meditation circles. With connections, both in Melbourne and the UK, Zooming together weekly supporting mindfulness. My spiritual family in Australia.

My two besties that I call sisters from another mother, Sue Lytollis and Andrea Cootes. Sue is my clubbing Sista and Andrea is my art Sista without sharing DNA. They open their hearts and share their families with me.

My techy friend who's too shy to be mentioned.

Maribyrnong libraries where I came across amazing inspirational books to read. The free events and workshops, like the writer's groups that meet monthly and book launches with live interviews with the authors. And the helpful team of supportive librarians.

And last, but not least, the amazing team at Ultimate 48 Hour Author, who have taken me to the finish line of publication. They have become my book family.

My website: heartstoriesdimsum.wordpress.com

www.ingramcontent.com/pod-product-compliance
Lightning Source LLC
Chambersburg PA
CBHW030053100526
44591CB00008B/125